ESCAPE TO THE SEA

Searching for the Good Life in Portugal

By the same author

ESCAPE TO THE HILLS

ESCAPE TO THE SEA

Searching for the Good Life in Portugal

Marie Wynne

Cover image:

AArcozelo (Vila Nova de Gaia). Joseolgon
26 July 2020, 16:57:14

To the future

‘Portuguese is cheerful and sweet,
like a language of birds.’

Paulo Rónai

PROLOGUE

The man was probably in his late seventies, or even early eighties. Either way, he shouldn't have been balanced on top of a ladder, stretching dangerously to a branch just beyond his reach. But I could see why. The cluster of ripe figs hanging there were fat and glowed purple in the afternoon sun. My mouth watered.

We had been happy to discover that our balcony looked out over the hotel's verdant garden. A couple of rickety looking garden chairs were the only nod to tourists; rather, it seemed a working garden, with rows of tall cabbages, staked tomato plants, and large fruit trees. My gaze swung anxiously again to the elderly gentleman in the fig tree. Luckily he hadn't fallen, but was now descending the ladder with a large basket of fruit. When he reached the bottom he placed the basket carefully on the ground and straightened his waistcoat.

I breathed in the warm air, which was fragrant with the scent of some unfamiliar bloom, and felt myself beginning to unwind. Beyond the garden, the spire of a church rose up to meet the heat haze and swallows wheeled over the terracotta roofs of ramshackle tenements.

I lifted my face to the sun and let it warm me. It was hard to believe that only that morning we had left an

English landscape brooding under heavy rain clouds. As the plane flew south, the skies had opened up to brilliant sunshine and we had felt ourselves relaxing. We were soon flying over a landscape of wooded valleys, vineyards, and isolated mountain villages, the colourful roof tiles vivid against a backdrop of green. As we began our descent over Porto, my stomach had lurched in excitement. The blue expanse of the sea filled the horizon, and then we saw the great curve of the River Douro, glinting in the sunshine.

In the taxi, a large beige Mercedes that had seen better days, we wound down the windows to breathe in the warm air. The fields lining the dusty roads were tall with yellow spears of corn. Unfamiliar scenes rolled past: jumbles of painted houses clustered around shadowy cobbled courtyards, strange billboards and shop fronts, and an occasional small field squeezed between apartment blocks and inhabited by sheep or goats. This felt more like South America than Europe.

I tore myself away from the view from the hotel balcony and slipped back into the dim coolness of our hotel room. It was time to explore, to make our first acquaintance with this strange city. We ventured out into the balmy September evening and wandered the city streets, charmed by the unfamiliar feel of cobbles underfoot. Each cafe and restaurant had its cluster of small tables spilling onto the bright cobbles, and scents of food and strong coffee wafted on the warm breeze. On a street corner, a woman with a brightly coloured headscarf was gutting sardines. The cleaned fish lay glinting in little boxes on her stall, for sale at a ridiculously low price. The woman smiled at us as we passed by.

In the UK, we had fled the city, supposedly for good. Now here we were, back in the middle of a big vibrant city, surrounded by people and bustle. But like Alice through the looking glass, we felt we had emerged into a parallel world. This was a city like no other we had experienced. Already, we were smitten. Could this become home?

1

I had been having a lovely dream. We were back in Porto, strolling by the river. There, right on the riverfront, was a large handsome house. Its terracotta roof tiles glowed in the sunshine and deep pink bougainvillea grew gracefully around the imposing front door. A white-haired old man, the man who I had spied picking figs from our hotel balcony, was standing in the doorway of the house smiling benevolently.

'How much is the house?' I asked him.

'It is a million euros,' he said. 'But to you, it is only two thousand euros.'

My heart sang. I shouted to Geoff, who for some reason had gone down to the water's edge to look for pebbles.

'We'll buy it now,' I told the old man. 'I just have to go and get my husband and sell our car to raise the money.'

'I can wait,' said the old man. 'I'll be here when you get back.'

I was telling Geoff the good news when I was wrenched cruelly out of sleep.

'Jeff!'

Silence.

'Jeff!'

Silence.

'Jeff! Gerrup you lazy sod, you're gonna be late!'

It was unfortunate that our next door neighbours had a teenage son called Jeff.

The dividing wall separating the two houses was thick but Carol's voice was like a foghorn.

'Jeff!'

'What?!'

'Gerrup!'

I sighed. Another rude awakening. Annoyingly, despite the din, my Geoff still slumbered beside me. I lay still and tried to catch the thread of the dream, willing myself back to Porto. But it was impossible. The cacophony of doors slamming in the street outside had rendered me fully awake. So I did what I often did in the mornings, I lay there and worried about work.

It dawned on me that it was a Thursday and my heart sank. I hated Thursdays. I had four 2-hour teaching sessions on Thursdays, and the 9 o'clock one was a Statistics class. Second-year psychology students faced with statistics early in the morning were liable to be grumpy and unresponsive, so the class was bound to be a barrel of laughs. I wouldn't even get a break at lunchtime as we had a staff meeting, so by early afternoon I would feel wrung out and the migraine I got every Thursday would have started to develop.

At the university where we both worked things had been feeling tense for a few years. A passion for psychology had prompted both of us to become academics, but ten years ago we had realized that the prospect of staying in the job for the twenty-five years it took to pay off a mortgage was distinctly unappealing. So we had taken the plunge and bought a remote, dilapidated little cottage with no mains services in the hills of Snowdonia in North Wales. Our plan was simple. We would renovate the cottage and live off-grid, making use of solar and wind power. We would try to grow all our own fruit and vegetables and be self-sufficient of the system.

Precisely because the cottage was small, remote, and dilapidated, it was cheap. We would pay it off as quickly as we could and live mortgage-free, with no bills for electricity, gas, or water. With few outgoings, we would be able to give up our stressful jobs at the university and enjoy instead the qualities we valued more: peace of mind and more time.

Readers of our first book, *Escape to the Hills*, will be familiar with the various successes and failures that characterized our efforts to escape the system. Suffice it to say that despite our efforts, this ideal lifestyle had not materialized. We had managed to make the cottage liveable and the garden productive. We had a basic system powered by solar panels and a wind turbine, and we had worked out a way to pump fresh spring water up to the cottage and to compost our own waste.

However, in the years we lived at the cottage, the weather had grown steadily worse, frustrating our attempts to develop our modest cottage economy. It felt like the wild landscape that we so loved was slowly reclaiming the cottage, making our hillside more and more unsuitable for human habitation. Added to that, the snow and torrential rain had made getting to work a feat of endurance and our health had suffered with the strain. And living off-grid had proved to be a lot more expensive than we had anticipated.

It was true that it felt liberating to have no monthly utility bills. However, we spent a huge amount each year on logs for the wood-burning stove. Another large expense was transport. Although we had converted our trusty Jeep 'Buffy' to LPG gas, she ate lots of fuel. Even if we hadn't been commuting regularly from North Wales to work, Buffy was essential. Our remote location and the lack of local facilities (the village shop had closed many years ago) meant that we couldn't avoid the expense of a reliable off-road vehicle.

We had realized part of our dream: we had managed to completely pay off our cottage. To the extent that we had no mortgage, we were free. However, we hadn't yet figured out an alternative source of income to enable us to finally give up our stressful jobs. We discovered that it was impossible to be self-sufficient in fruit and vegetables while battling gale force winds and almost constant rain. And without our own woodland, we couldn't produce our own firewood.

So we had reluctantly accepted that it would be some years before we could cast off the shackles of work. In the meantime, we badly needed a bolthole in the city within a reasonable commuting distance to work. The solution was to do what we had vowed never to do again: to get a mortgage and buy another house. This time, however, it would be different. We would renovate the house and rent out rooms. The top floor of the property, which we nicknamed the Halfway House, had already been converted into a small bedsit, which we could live in when we weren't at the cottage.

In theory, it seemed ideal. In practice, things hadn't worked out as planned (what does?). Staying in Liverpool during the week had certainly cut down the stress and expense of travelling to and from Wales. The trouble was, we were now spending most weekends in the city because of the wild weather, hiding from the damp and cold of the cottage. It wasn't the solution we had hoped for. We needed to escape — from our jobs, from the city, and from the weather. So, just as we had finally finished renovating the Halfway House and were ready to advertise for tenants, we tossed all our original plans in the air and decided to move to Portugal.

Geoff stirred beside me, finally roused by the din of slamming car doors. Next door had obviously managed to extract their Jeff from his bed and were beginning the school run. They had only moved in three weeks ago but already they were making the street their own. Our previous loutish neighbours, who had been nicknamed the Clampetts by our builder, had moved out. Unfortunately, they had been replaced by a family so uncannily similar that we had named them the NeoClampetts. Like the original Clampetts, the newcomers were goodhearted but loud, very loud. Perhaps it is an unwritten law of the universe that dictates that like must be replaced with like. A balance must be kept. Or maybe both sets of neighbours were sent to teach us tolerance and restraint. Either way, they were hard to live with.

I estimated about two more minutes before the wretched alarm went off and the morning rush started. I wished we were in Portugal. But, I reflected, that wasn't going to happen any time soon. We had worked out that we could sell the cottage and probably afford to buy a cheap house or apartment in Portugal. But we had debts to pay off too. Exploring a personal interest in Chinese medicine, we had both spent the last three years completing a part-time course in acupuncture, funded by career development loans. We had yet to pay those off.

More importantly, what would we live on if we moved to Portugal? We needed money behind us while we found jobs over there or figured out an alternative way of supporting ourselves. So in a way, we were back where we had started. We needed to pay off the mortgage on the Halfway House so that we could sell it and obtain enough money to live on until we had settled in Portugal and established a secure income. We reasoned that if we lived like monks we could pay off the house in ten years, maybe eight. It was a long time to wait. Sometimes, especially on a Thursday, it seemed interminable.

Still, we had discovered a way of bringing the Portugal dream a little closer. Several Portuguese estate agents had websites, and some were in English. At weekends, we cheered ourselves up by scouring these sites for likely candidates for our new home. We had no Internet connection at the cottage, but we found a workaround. If we were in Wales for the weekend, we drove into Llandudno on Saturdays to shop for groceries, calling at Glynis' laundry in Llanrwst first (running large devices like washing machines was beyond our small off-grid system). We then spent the afternoons in the local fast-food restaurant using their free Wi-Fi. Hunched over laptops, the rain beating down on the windows, we consoled ourselves by scrolling through pages of sun-drenched pictures of derelict stone cottages and romantic ruined *quintas*. Trying to ignore the noise of small children shouting and throwing chips on the floor (and at each other), we drank strong tea and dreamed.

We found another good source of comfort in the form of Internet blogs written by folks who were also planning a move to Portugal. The country was starting to acquire a reputation as a warm, safe, and inexpensive place to emigrate to, and it seemed that lots of people were keen to document their experiences of fleeing to Portugal in search of a better life. Following other people's preparations and adventures made the dream feel a little closer. As well as providing vicarious enjoyment, the blogs were a good source of information (not always reliable) on topics such as the requirements for moving permanently to the country and the best Portuguese language resources.

However, our browsing sessions often left us dissatisfied. Many of the bloggers were on the final countdown to emigrating. They had reached the exciting parts of the process, such as house-hunting. We, on the other hand, had years to endure before we could even think about where in the country we might live, let alone what kind of house we could afford. And it seemed that everyone had more money than we were likely to have. For instance, one family who planned to move to a villa in the Algarve were taxed trying to decide what shape swimming pool to have. It was a problem we were unlikely to face. A couple who blogged about their imminent move to Lisbon wondered about whether to save up for a six- or seven-bedroom townhouse. Although as the same couple seemed to spend most of their house-hunting trips staying in expensive five star hotels and going for slap-up meals, we suspected it might take them rather longer than they planned to reach their savings goal.

Then one day we had an idea. We came across an estate agent that specialized in rural Portuguese properties in need of renovation. Some were partly renovated or had planning permission but others were full projects. And they were very cheap. We spent an excited afternoon poring over the website and bookmarking possible properties. What we needed, we reasoned, was somewhere just like our Welsh cottage, but in the sun. A dilapidated cottage or barn in the middle of nowhere would be perfect. We could take our time renovating it, save up for building materials and do the work slowly. This revelation opened up new possibilities. The estate agent listings included picturesque ruins, rustic barns, and tiny hovels, often with acres of land attached. And prices were as low as ten thousand euros. If we could save up a little more, maybe twenty or thirty thousand euros, we might be able to buy a piece of paradise sooner than we thought.

We clung to the possibility all through a dispiriting winter term at the university. The weather was atrocious, and we managed only occasional visits to Wales to check that the cottage was alright. Our cat Bibby sulked constantly at being wrenched from his Welsh hillside and confined to the Halfway House. Guiltily, we bought him a new cat bed and placed it in a cosy corner of the sitting room. However, Bibby took up residence under the coffee table and refused to be budged.

'Do you think he can sense something we can't?' I asked Geoff one day.

'What do you mean?'

'Well, maybe he can detect a ley line, or a power spot or something,' I suggested. 'There must be some reason for him choosing to sit there instead of in his bed.'

Geoff moved a protesting Bibby aside to examine the favoured spot. Then he grinned.

'Typical! I know why the little rotter's sitting here.'

'Why?'

'Come and feel this carpet.'

I went and placed my hand on the spot where Bibby had been sitting.

'It's so warm! Has he got a temperature?'

'No he hasn't. He's managed to locate the exact spot where the hot water pipe feeding the radiator runs under the floorboards!'

And so he had. He spent the winter comforting himself with his underfloor heating and we didn't blame him for it.

We consoled ourselves with sporadic bouts of gardening in the tiny back garden. We had managed to squeeze into the limited space a couple of vegetable beds to grow garlic, squash, and tomatoes. The old brick wall that surrounded the garden provided a sheltered environment and the plants grew well enough. But it wasn't exactly a haven of tranquillity. Even if you hid under the weeping willow at the bottom of the garden you could hear the noise of the nearby expressway. And the NeoClampetts contributed their own particular soundscape. The thud-thud of the youngest son's football against the shared brick wall perfectly complimented the constant churn of the cement mixer in the backyard. Vince had poked his head over the wall to introduce himself and had confided to us his plans to concrete over the soil in their back garden and install a gas barbecue.

'You don't like plants then?' asked Geoff.

'Nah,' replied Vince. 'They make too much mess. Carol likes 'em, she keeps bringing plants home. But I move them!' Smiling, he surveyed the tangle of edible and ornamental plants in our own garden. 'Are they weeds?' He pointed to a large clump of Italian meadow rocket.

Geoff pulled off some leaves and handed them to Vince. 'It's rocket,' he said. 'We use it in salads. Try some — it's really nice.'

Vince looked at the rocket leaves doubtfully. 'I don't eat green things,' he said.

But he followed Geoff's example and shoved a few leaves in his mouth. He chewed apprehensively then screwed up his face in distaste. 'Ugh!' he grimaced. 'Give me a burger any day, mate!' He said a hasty goodbye and went back to his cement mixer.

When we had bought our first house together, over a decade ago, we had quickly felt trapped by the thought of spending forty years in a stressful job just to pay off the mortgage. Now we were back in the same position: trying to escape from the city, from work, from the system. But until we could raise some money, we were stuck. And that meant that for now, we had to put up with the NeoClampetts and their enthusiastic but noisy home improvements. They had ripped out their kitchen and were in the process of installing a new one. Carol had explained to us, somewhat gleefully we thought, that because they had no cooking facilities they had to go to the nearby burger joint for all their meals. Which at least got them out of the house, and out of earshot, three times a day.

But the NeoClampetts were a good source of amusing stories about our old neighbours the Clampetts. One day, Carol showed us their staircase, from which they had removed the wood laminate flooring the Clampetts had fitted. Carol and Vince had been shocked to discover that underneath the flooring, the stairs were carpeted. Rather than remove the old, stained carpet, the Clampetts had simply fitted the new flooring on top of it.

Curious about what had become of our old neighbours, Geoff asked Carol one day where they had moved to. After selling their house, the Clampetts had apparently moved 'up North,' according to Carol. They had bought a long-stay mobile home on a holiday park and had promptly been thrown out for antisocial behaviour. No, she didn't know where they were now, but (and she lowered her voice to a whisper) she had been careful to change the locks on the front door just in case!

2

Sitting over our simple-looking food in the simple-looking restaurant we had selected, we reflected that in Portugal, appearances could be deceptive. We had left our charming hotel and wandered through the soft September evening to a pretty tree-lined square. The street was pedestrianized, so it had the quiet, relaxed bustle that occurs when people can walk through a beautiful city without having to constantly dodge cars. Everything was deliciously different: the feel of cobbles rather than tarmac under our sandals, the warm fragrant air, the little eddies of Portuguese conversation drifting out of open doors and windows.

We sat in the square for a while, listening to the birds in the trees and watching a group of elderly men sat around a card table talking and smoking. Then we wandered past the cafes and restaurants that clustered round the square, peeking into dimly lit interiors and appraising menus carefully. After all, this would be our very first meal together in Portugal. It felt momentous somehow.

We finally chose an unassuming place called Romero's, which was opposite an old-fashioned tailor's shop that was straight out of the 1950s. The restaurant's sign was faded and the paint on the shutters was peeling a little, but it had a good feel. We ventured inside and found ourselves in a long, dim interior. The restaurant seemed empty, but as we gazed round we heard a friendly '*Ola!*' from the back of the room. Behind a huge wooden serving bar a woman was busy stacking plates. She smiled and gestured for us to choose a table.

The wooden furniture was dated but the white tablecloths were linen and spotless. The ceiling was crisscrossed with wooden beams to which were fixed decorative brass anchors and fish, and the walls were elaborately tiled with scenes of fishing boats and harbours.

Perusing the menu, we realized we had stumbled into what was essentially a fish restaurant. We should have known from the decor. When the smiling waitress appeared we confessed our vegetarian status. She shrugged expansively.

'Is okay,' she said. 'We can make you another thing.'

Her father, we learnt, was the chef and apparently he made a mean ham and mushroom omelette. We agreed enthusiastically.

'Without the ham,' Geoff reminded her.

She nodded. 'And something to drink?'

She disappeared to talk to her father and fetch the wine.

We hadn't ordered a starter so when she reappeared and placed a generous basket of bread and a large platter of olives and cheese on the table we were surprised.

'*Couvert*,' she explained. 'Only pay for what you eat. My father says you are sure you don't want just a little bit of ham? It is from the Alentejo.'

We were sure.

We couldn't resist sampling the *couvert*. The bread was deliciously fresh and the cheese full and creamy. The olives were incredible.

'Do you think it would be crazy to move to Portugal just for the olives?' Geoff said.

'No,' I said firmly.

Our omelettes, when they came, were fluffy and delicious (and thankfully ham-free). They were served on enormous plates that also held a heap of *batatas fritas* (French fries), rice, and a colourful salad. In contrast to the half-hearted restaurant side salads we were used to, which usually consisted of a limp lettuce leaf or two adorned by a couple of anaemic tomato slices, this was an eclectic mix of shredded carrot, large chunks of tomato, and fat olives. The rice, which is often served alongside fries, was subtle but delicious. When Geoff asked the waitress what was in the rice she told us it was 'the usual.' When pressed for details, she was unable to tell us, beyond salt and pepper, as she didn't know the English words for the ingredients.

The bottle of *vinho verde*, Portugal's sparkling young ('green') wine, was one of the cheapest on the menu but was outstanding. It was crisp and fruity and we sipped it and marvelled. This trip to Porto had been a good idea, we decided. Slogging through the autumn term, dreaming of one day escaping to the sun, it had seemed like a sign when we had heard of an interesting conference in Porto, Portugal's second biggest city. It seemed like a good opportunity for what would be our first trip to Portugal together. The university usually paid for staff to attend conferences but only if you had been invited to give a paper. We hadn't, so we would have to fund the trip ourselves. But we didn't care; it was the excuse we needed to fit in a quick reconnaissance trip.

The conference began on our first full day in Porto, and we dutifully turned up at the venue and sat through the morning sessions. The talks were interesting enough, but we were both uncharacteristically fidgety and restless. We were finally in Portugal. What were we doing in a stuffy lecture room? There was a whole city out there waiting to be explored! At lunchtime, we fled the conference.

We wandered downhill to the Ribeira, the old riverside quarter. Here, the colourful houses rose up the hillside, piled high like layer upon layer of confectionary. We loved the lack of uniformity; some buildings had been lovingly refurbished, their painted mouldings bright like icing on a wedding cake, their tiled frontages and neat shutters gleaming. Others — and we liked these the best — were neglected and empty, their shutters faded and their garrets roofed by worn tin sheeting.

Strolling past the old oak doors of these unloved dwellings we discovered a curious thing. Many of the doors had gaps or open letterboxes through which drifted out the most extraordinary scent. It was a mixture of old, old wood and damp, but the result was an evocative smell, for all the world like a rich frankincense. As we walked the city, we found ourselves seeking out old buildings and wandering slowly past their decaying portals, sniffing the air for the hint of frankincense. The novelist Marcel Proust, when assailed by the scent of madeleine cake dipped in tea, was instantly transported back through the years to Sunday mornings at his Aunt Léonie's house. Even now, years later, that faint incense aroma caught when hurrying past an old house never fails to evoke for us that first magical visit.

Sitting on the terrace of a cafe on the Ribeira sipping cold beer, we made a decision. We would play truant from the conference and spend the week exploring. We wanted to soak up the atmosphere, to bask in the scents of the city and the sea, to feel the sun on our backs. More importantly, we needed to find out if the feel of the place, of this country that was so old but so new to us, was right. In other words, did it feel like it could become home?

Porto is not a large city. It covers only about forty-one

square kilometres, which makes it ideal for exploring on foot. That first week, it felt like we walked most of the city. We revelled in being completely unfamiliar with the place and wandered through many areas well off the usual tourist path.

One day, we took the Metro and got off randomly at Heroísmo station. We wandered past workaday apartment blocks, flower shops, and pharmacies to find ourselves outside a huge old cemetery. Within its gates, the elaborate tombs and ancient trees seemed to generate a hush that was a world away from the city bustle.

Emerging, we sought the cool of a cafe that was so tiny it contained only three small tables arranged in a galley-like space. The elderly couple behind the counter looked a little nervous at the prospect of serving two *estrangeiros*, but we managed to order freshly squeezed orange juice and cake in Portuguese. Suitably refreshed, we started heading back to the Metro station when we heard someone calling behind us. We turned to see the woman from the cafe hastily pursuing us; we had left our camera in the cafe and she was anxious to return it.

Wandering through the Lapa district one afternoon, we were intrigued by the entrance to a narrow alleyway filled with potted plants. It looked like a plant nursery or garden centre so we ventured down. The alley gave on to a large walled garden filled with plants of many different types. They sat in huge terracotta pots against the walls, cascaded down from hanging baskets, spilled out of old wheelbarrows and repurposed paint cans. For plant lovers like ourselves it was heaven. But then Geoff nudged me.

'Do you notice anything?'

'What do you mean?'

'There are no signs or anything. I don't think these plants are for sale!'

He was right. This wasn't a shop. It looked like we had stumbled into somebody's garden. As we started to back out, we noticed someone waving at us. An elderly gentleman had paused in his task of pruning an olive tree and was beckoning us. Our Portuguese was limited to greetings, apologies, and some cafe-related words and he obviously spoke no English. But he proceeded with smiles to show us some of his choice specimens, waving away our apologies for trespassing, carefully repeating the Portuguese terms for the plants, and patiently listening to our fumbled pronunciation.

We continued wandering aimlessly, being drawn from one sight to another, a kind of therapy in itself. Before leaving Lapa we stopped at a fruit shop, attracted by the golden peaches displayed in a box outside. We chose two and entered the shop to pay. We were surprised when the proprietor asked us if the peaches were to eat now. When we nodded, she placed them on the counter and took us to another box of peaches of a different variety. She chose two, earnestly explaining that these were much tastier than the ones we had chosen. We were touched at her concern that we had the very best eating experience. And it was. Both of us have never forgotten the amazing scent and taste of those juicy peaches. We were beginning to experience and enjoy the gentle concern that the Portuguese paid even to strangers.

On the way back to the hotel we paused to stare at Lapa's huge and beautiful church. As we gazed, a tiny old lady appeared from a side street and headed for the church. She was carrying a large plastic box, and as she neared the church steps a multitude of cats appeared from all directions. She was obviously on time tonight; the cats were ready and waiting. Soon the woman was surrounded by felines who proceeded to yowl at her quite mercilessly.

She opened her box and liberally scattered what we assumed to be cat biscuits over the steps, then stood and watched happily while her charges feasted. Like so many of our experiences that week, the sight was unexpected, simple, but beautiful.

Although we were drawn to the merits of buying a cheap house in the countryside in Portugal, we began to be seduced by Porto. The city was a huge draw, and we couldn't help feeling that it would be good to live at least within driving distance of the place. So we decided to explore some of the towns and villages in the countryside near Porto.

The next day we took the Metro out to Vila do Conde, a seaside town not far from Porto. In an almost empty carriage, we sat and watched the city outskirts quickly give way to countryside. We gazed wonderingly at the railway embankments, which were crowded with wild fig trees, vines, and blue convolvulus. We pointed out to each other the colourful allotments that lined the railway. We glimpsed sweetcorn, orange trees, chickens. We caught an instant of one scene, frozen like a tableau as the train sped us past, of two men in the act of slaughtering a goat. It was a far cry from Merseyside. Everything seemed more real, direct, and down to earth than it did in modern Britain.

At Vila do Conde we wandered around, breathing in the salty air. We admired the long sandy beaches and watched the Portuguese families crowding the sea-front cafes, eating, drinking, smoking, and laughing, seemingly deeply at ease. Wandering on, we selected our own cafe, and ate freshly made pizza in a sun-drenched square near a fountain, then walked back to the beach to drench our tired feet in the cold Atlantic waves. We were slowing down, and beginning to understand the Iberian attitude that nothing is so urgent that it cannot wait until tomorrow.

Although we had only a week we wanted to check out as much of the region as possible. The next day we took the mainline train to Coimbra, a university town to the south of Porto. Although smaller than Porto, Coimbra is also a river town, and its historical heart is centred on the university old town. We climbed up to the university quarter through a steep maze of narrow alleys and cobbled steps. Here, the old walls of the sun-baked little lanes were bright with thoughtful graffiti, some of it fiercely critical of meat eating. Vegetarianism and veganism was obviously becoming more popular with the students, if not with older generations.

We sank down gratefully at a cafe with a spectacular view. The waiter, a large middle-aged man with an impressive moustache, handed us menus and began to describe the dish of the day. When we told him that we didn't eat meat and asked if there were any vegetarian dishes he stared at us with a mixture of pity and disbelief.

'Não carne?' he repeated.

We shook our heads. He looked nonplussed but then he brightened.

'Não problema!' He pointed out the section on the menu that listed the fish dishes.

We explained that we didn't eat fish either.

'Não carne, não peixe?' he said, trying to conceal his disbelief.

A little embarrassed, we confirmed this sad state of affairs.

This floored the poor man. He stood and shook his head sadly, repeating 'Não carne, não peixe!'

He eventually shrugged his shoulders and apologized. He could offer no suggestions, he said. The cafe did not serve vegetarian food. He wished he could help us but if we refused to eat carne or peixe ... His kindly face wrinkled into a worried frown. What about *um café e uma nata*?

To save his feelings, we accepted coffee and custard tarts then, freaks that we were, we slunk away to try our luck elsewhere. The university students might have been slowly changing their eating habits, but some of the cafes were yet to follow.

We seemed to have developed a particular talent for scaring waiters that week. We took the train to Braga, a city north of Portugal, and famous for its cathedral. We strolled through its smart streets and admired the well-stocked delicatessens before turning off into the side streets to explore the city in more depth. We made a beeline for a cafe with an elaborate wrought iron sign and window-boxes full of flowers. Taking a table, we browsed the menus.

After about fifteen minutes, nobody had come to take our order, which we thought was strange, as the cafe was not particularly busy. We had both noticed a man lurking in a dark corner behind the counter and occasionally shooting us suspicious glances. Eventually, we heard a woman's voice from the back of the shop, raised as if in a gentle reprimand, and Lurker reluctantly approached our table. He readied his notebook and with downcast eyes asked us what we wanted. In our pidgin Portuguese we managed to order some food. Having written down our order, Lurker visibly relaxed.

The woman who brought our food greeted us gaily in English and then apologized for not being more fluent. We had started to get used to such apologies, which were usually given in almost flawless English, and always made us feel guilty about our pitiful grasp of Portuguese. She put down our plates then nodded towards the counter, where Lurker was watching us apprehensively.

'He's terrified of you!' she giggled. 'He knew when you

came in that you weren't Portuguese. But he doesn't speak English so he was too scared to come and serve you.'

However, when we went to the counter to pay, and asked Lurker how to correctly pronounce '*dinheiro*,' he actually smiled. By the time we left, he was positively cheerful and even managed, with the help of his boss, to wish us a hesitant 'Good-afternoon-have-a-nice-day.'

On our last night in Porto, our feet were so sore from a week of walking we looked for the closest restaurant to the hotel. Just off Rua de Cedofeita, we were attracted by an atmospherically lit place hidden away down a flight of stone steps. Too tired to really care what kind of food it served we stumbled down the steps and into a small room that looked a most unpromising venue for a restaurant. However, we had managed to find a little gem. Not only did the place serve imaginatively cooked vegetarian food but it also had a peaceful courtyard filled with plants. We ate under an indigo sky surrounded by the scent of wisteria.

After our meal, we called for the last time at 'our' local cafe. We had discovered at the beginning of the week that there was no kettle in our room. As we both liked a cup of herbal tea before bed, I ventured down to reception to ask for some hot water to make tea with. The obliging receptionist ushered me through to the kitchen and left me with the cook, who she instructed to get me some hot water. The cook was a chatty lady who seemed delighted to have a guest in her kitchen. She showed me the collection of pot plants that adorned the kitchen windowsill and then insisted that I sit in her armchair while she fetched me the water. As I watched, she took a large glazed jug and filled it with tap water, carefully running the water first until it was hot. Beaming, she handed me the jug. In vain, I tried to explain that we wanted boiling water for the tea, but my attempts at Portuguese and her attempts at English baffled us both. She had been so kind I was loathe to hurt her feelings. I thanked her profusely for the water and fled back to our room.

After that, we gave up on the mission for hot water. Coffee is king in Portugal and I think the hotel just assumed that the rare guest who wanted tea would simply find a cafe and order some. So that was what we did. We finished off each evening by calling at a small cafe just round the corner from the hotel and ordering a pot of the popular *cidreira* tea, made from the flowers of the herb lemon balm. The cafe owners must have been Brazilian, because faded posters of Brazil adorned the walls, the theme broken only by a worn poster of Che Guevara. Sitting each evening at the same rickety formica table underneath Che Guevara, we swapped our impressions of the city and wracked our brains for ideas about how we could fast-track our move to Portugal.

3

You know that moment in the film when Dorothy lands in Oz, and the dowdy monochrome of Kansas is replaced by the glorious Technicolor of Oz? Well, that was how we felt, but in reverse, when we returned to the UK from that first visit to Portugal. Being back under cool cloudy skies after a week in sun-drenched Porto was, quite frankly, rather distressing.

En route back to the cottage, we visited a supermarket in Llandudno to stock up on food. We trawled round the shop moodily, remembering how vibrant and cheap the produce in Portugal had been and making unfavourable comparisons with what was on offer on the supermarket shelves. Walking round the supermarket, and later through the streets of Llandudno, one of the differences that hit me most was the lack of smells. Wandering through Porto, we had been constantly assailed by interesting scents. Strolling past the little grocery shops, the scent of fresh fruit and slabs of dried *bacalhau* (dried salted codfish) drifted out of doorways and the rich smell of food cooked over charcoal grills in the *churrasqueira* restaurants filled the streets. The scent of the river, and over it all, a hint of the nearby sea as a constant presence, like the guardian spirit of the city.

Daily life in the UK suddenly seemed to lack colour, scent, and flavour. We wanted to wander through warm cobbled streets and do our shopping in bustling markets and fragrant bakeries. But the local shop in our village in North Wales had been closed for decades, and a stroll down the dual carriageway near our Liverpool house, should you be able to stand the petrol fumes, led only to a large supermarket. Many of the artisan shops and markets we remembered from our childhoods had been replaced by chain stores and shopping malls. Any cobbles had long been covered by tarmac and the small bars turned into theme pubs. It all seemed so packaged, so sterile.

Sometimes, when we had stayed over at the cottage (which was increasingly rare) and had to commute to work, we stopped for breakfast at a supermarket that shall remain nameless. In their depressing cafe we ordered eggs and toast. The bread was always under-toasted, to the extent that it was almost too limp to pick up off the plate. The eggs were similarly anaemic, and the service was grumpy to the point of hostility. We always moaned to each other about the disappointing experience but as there were no small cafes left in the area, we always went back. The food reeked of tight margins and exploited kitchen staff. No wonder it was almost inedible.

We had come to realize that our move to North Wales had been a search for a time, rather than a place. Jaded with the stress of modern urban life and firmly shackled to the hamster wheel of an endless round of work, mortgage payments, and commuting, we had sought a simpler, more authentic way of life. But this had proved surprisingly elusive. It dawned on us that perhaps the type of lifestyle we craved no longer existed in the UK, if it ever had.

There is a term in Portuguese that is almost untranslatable.

Saudade has been described as a nostalgic yearning or melancholic longing, often for something or someone that is unattainable. The concept is very similar to the Welsh concept of *hiraeth*. In 1912, the scholar Aubrey Bell described the feeling of *saudade* as 'a vague and constant desire for something that does not and probably cannot exist, for something other than the present.' Was that what we had been doing; running after a dream that didn't exist, trying to return to an ideal past and escape our modern-day responsibilities? If so, we were still running.

But Portugal seemed to offer an escape. There, we had felt that the remnants of an older way of life still existed. In the warmth of the people, the concern about good food, even the old men playing cards in the little squares, we sensed that those characteristics central to quality of life, such as community and connection with the land, were still important in Portugal. And we felt more alive there.

Unfortunately, we had to live in the present and face reality. And it was depressing. Work was particularly difficult, as the university was going through a period of intense change. There were constant battles between the union and the management over pay and working conditions, frequent strikes, and an atmosphere of ill-will all round.

We cheered ourselves up by making weekend pilgrimages to Wrexham, where we had discovered a Portuguese cafe. Here, we could indulge our taste for aromatic coffee and *pasteis de nata* and practice our Portuguese on the bemused owner. Whenever we called there, the place was packed with Portuguese people sitting in their coats in a fug of heat over coffee and cake. The television was usually on to allow the glum customers to gaze longingly at images of sun-drenched Portuguese beaches. We knew how they felt.

We also took solace in searching for properties on

Portuguese websites and trying to learn the language. We read up on the characteristics of the different regions of Portugal. Although the countryside around Porto was the likely favourite, we wondered whether we should explore other areas before deciding where to settle. After all, it was a big decision.

Although Portugal is a relatively small country, it encompasses a variety of different landscapes and climates. The central and southern regions are hotter and drier and the northern parts cooler and wetter in winter. The Moors invaded Portugal in the 8th century CE, and the southern and central areas of the country show more evidence of a Moorish influence in the architecture and cuisine. Geoff had visited the Algarve many years ago and had liked the area, but we worried that the south might be too hot for us. We were used to the mountains of North Wales; a climate that was very hot and dry would probably be too much of a shock to our systems!

We liked the fact that, like Wales, Portugal has a strong Celtic heritage, particularly in the north. In fact, one of the earliest settlements in Portugal was probably on the banks of the River Douro, in what is now Vila Nova de Gaia, in the Porto district. The name of this settlement was Portus Cale; the word *Cale* or *Cailleach* is thought to be the name of a Celtic goddess. The term Portus Cale later mutated into Portugal and was used to refer to the whole country rather than just the region around the Douro, with *Cale* becoming *Gaia*.

Our research suggested that the landscape of the north of Portugal was similar to that of Wales, so we were likely to feel at home there. And there seemed to be lots of affordable properties for sale in the mountains. However, much as we loved living in the mountains of Snowdonia, the life was hard. We had had our fill of wild winds and torrential rain. We needed an easier climate.

It felt good having narrowed down our options to the north. But we still had to decide exactly where to settle. Over the next year we made another two trips to Porto. We decided to try and get a different perspective on the city by renting out accommodation rather than staying in hotels.

On one trip we stayed in a small apartment in a beautiful old building on the Ribeira. We had a spectacular view of the river and were in the midst of the lively bustle of the popular riverside quarter. A bit too in the midst. Every night, the accordion player at the restaurant just across the square loudly serenaded the guests, and every night we lay awake until midnight cursing him.

After he left, there would be a brief lull during which we would finally doze off, only to be violently awakened in the early hours by the sound of all the nearby restaurants throwing their empty bottles into the recycling bins. I seem to remember our explorations on that particular trip as being befuddled by sleeplessness.

But I will never forget an experience I had one night in that apartment. I was lying in bed wide awake, partly because of the bloody accordion player but also due to the effects of being in the sun all day. We had begun to wonder if Portuguese people seem to need so little sleep because of the energizing effects of the sun and their excellent diet. That night, I wasn't particularly tired, and lay listening to the hum of the city. Suddenly, a thought popped unbidden into my mind: I was listening to the beating heart of the city. It was odd, and in the morning it seemed a bit fanciful, but at that moment I felt the beginnings of a deep sense of connection with Porto.

On our next trip we stayed in what we hoped would be a quieter location. We rented an old town house in the centre of the city, near the historic and vibrant Rua de

Santa Catarina, one of the main shopping thoroughfares of Porto. Like the Ribeira apartment, the house had lovely original features, such as traditional wooden shutters. It also had a pretty courtyard. It was a delight to walk to the nearby shops to buy fresh produce, prepare our meals in the beautiful tiled kitchen, and then eat in the courtyard on a table set underneath the orange tree. We drank locally produced wine and pretended that this was our house and that we were in Portugal for good.

On these visits, we left the city on reconnaissance trips to likely areas for future exploration. We figured that if we could decide on a general area that felt right, we could come back and hire a car to explore the countryside in more depth and to check out the villages in the area.

We took the train to Aveiro, a city set on a large lagoon. The train wound past sand dunes and salt marshland alive with herons and other wading birds. We ate lunch in a sunny square lined with Art Nouveau-style houses and gazed up at the storks' nests perched precariously on chimney pots and the top of telegraph poles. Aveiro is crisscrossed with canals and is sometimes called the Venice of Portugal. After lunch, we wandered alongside the canals and admired the colourful *barcos*, the traditional barges.

We also visited Viana do Castelo, a town on the banks of the River Lima. Viana is small but perfectly formed. Its cobbled streets are picture-perfect, its history and architecture impressive, and its closeness to the sea tempting. In Viana's genteel squares, people sat at tables quietly sipping wine and dogs dozed on the church steps. Surely this was ideal? We tried to imagine living in a village near Viana, driving into town for supplies and a dose of culture. But we couldn't.

We were surprised at how smaller the cities and towns are in Portugal. In the UK, even relatively small towns are surrounded by extensive urban sprawl. In Portugal, the urban centres quickly give way to countryside, so even major towns can feel compact and relatively rural. We were used to rural, we liked rural. And we had planned to search for a new home that, like our Welsh cottage, was romantically remote. But, disconcertingly, we realized our feelings had changed. The more we explored other locations, the more we realized how much we liked Porto. It had to be the city or nothing. The problem was, a home in or near Porto would cost a lot more than a tumbledown cottage in the countryside. Still, we were going to be in the UK for at least another eight years while we saved up enough money to move.

But then, suddenly, we weren't. At work, the union and the management had reached a rapprochement. Generous voluntary redundancy packages would be offered. I think the management hoped that the staff who had been there longest (and hence were more expensive) would fall on the sword, so to speak, and disappear. We were happy to. The sudden prospect of an early release was like the answer to a prayer. However, there was a downside. We now had only a year to find a home in Portugal, pay off everything we owed, and sell two houses. In a recession.

If we could pull it off, we knew this would be our best chance to make an escape. So we threw ourselves into paying off all our debts and selling everything we weren't going to take to Portugal, which was about three-quarters of our possessions. We had been shocked at how high shipping costs were. It would be cheaper to buy furniture and white goods in Portugal after the move, rather than paying a fortune to take everything with us. Besides, it wasn't like we had lots of expensive antiques or heirlooms. To keep costs down, we had used mostly second-hand furniture, sometimes donated by family, to furnish the

Halfway House. We had one or two pieces at the cottage, but these would have to be transported to Liverpool on or in Buffy.

The thing we had most of was books. As academics, books were a passion and our stock in trade and we had hundreds of them, both in our offices at work and at home. Books were heavy, and so would be expensive to transport. Most of them had to go, and it made sense to try and sell them, as we would need all the money we could get to start our new life. We therefore spent weeks listing and selling as many books as we could online. The Halfway House looked like a weird chaotic bookshop, with files of catalogued books and packages waiting to be posted.

With both the Halfway House and the cottage now on the market we had to move fast to find a suitable property in Porto. We had planned to return to Portugal a few more times and hire a car to explore the countryside around Porto. But there was no time for that now. To speed things up, we decided to look for a place in the city, even it was just a tiny apartment. It would be a base or a stepping stone; once we had made the move we could look for somewhere bigger if funds allowed. We had to avoid renting at all costs; it would eat up our budget and then we would never be able to afford to buy a place.

We worked out that selling the cottage and the Halfway House would probably raise enough to buy a small house or apartment outright in Portugal. And we could use our redundancy pay to live on for a couple of years while we figured out a way to make some money. It would be tight, but it would be do-able.

We began searching estate agents' websites with a vengeance, bookmarking likely properties. But our tiny budget meant that there weren't many to bookmark. We were working with an absolute maximum of eighty thousand euros, with a sincere hope that we could find something a lot cheaper than that. Although our initial plan had been to purchase a total renovation project, we soon abandoned this idea. Buying a cheap ruin was all well and good, but how easy would it be to organize major building work in a new country when we knew nothing about the building and planning laws and couldn't speak the language? Our Welsh cottage had required work, but it was liveable when we bought it. True, we had lived by candlelight and had no bathroom, but we spent some of the week in a heated office in the university and had a circle of friends and family to support us. Living like peasants in Portugal would be a very different prospect.

We needed somewhere we could move into, even if it was a little primitive. Adding the requirement of structural soundness reduced the number of potentially suitable properties alarmingly. However, we managed to find a handful of possible candidates and set about contacting estate agents. It is a curious fact that many estate agents in Portugal do not provide a full description of each property they are advertising. We came across listings that showed just one or two photos of a property, and some even showed only the garden, or a back view of the house. Unfortunately, this simply allows the imagination of a potential buyer to run wild, and conjure up all sorts of dire reasons to explain the missing information. Although we tried to avoid such listings, those we eventually selected had rather miserly descriptions to say the least.

For example, our front runner was a little house in Vila Nova de Gaia that seemed to have a view of the River Douro and a small garden. But the estate agent hadn't thought to state whether the Riverside House, as we referred to it, was detached, semi-detached, or terraced. Similarly, none of the photos showed the house from the road, so it wasn't clear what the area was like. For all we knew, the house might be next door to an abattoir.

All we could do was arrange some viewings and hope for the best. We had assumed that our budget would stretch only to apartments, so were surprised to find that were at least a few affordable houses. We just hoped they didn't turn out to be building sites. Most of the properties we found, including our favourite, the Riverside House, were listed with the same estate agent, so we contacted them first. We decided to send an email in English but include a Portuguese translation to be safe. Accordingly, we used a translation website to generate what we hoped was an understandable message, giving the dates we would be visiting Porto and asking if we could arrange some viewings.

The response that came back was prompt, friendly, and in English. But it mystified us. It seemed to be from a man who called himself Pedro Little Chicken. He was delighted, he said, to receive our email and would be very happy to show us round some houses. We had asked specifically whether the Riverside House was detached and its general position. Pedro said he was pleased to tell us that the house had four frontages and was next to a washing machine. Hmmm. It seemed we weren't the only ones who had used online translation, and fallen foul of its tendency for over-literal language conversion. We dreaded to think of the pidgin Portuguese we had probably inflicted on the poor Mr Little Chicken. It promised to be an interesting house-hunt.

4

Two days before we were due to fly to Portugal to look for a new home, we sold the cottage. We took the bus into Liverpool city centre and celebrated with a meal at Villa Romana, our favourite Italian restaurant. The September evening was cold so we asked for a table near the fire. Over freshly made pizza and a bottle of good Valpolicella, we collected our thoughts. With the sale of the cottage, we were a little closer to our dream of moving to Portugal. But we still had the Halfway House to sell. If it didn't sell quickly, the mortgage payments would rapidly consume our redundancy money. But if it did sell quickly, we would be homeless. So the pressure was now on to find a home in Portugal. The choice of homes available at our meagre budget wasn't exactly huge, but at least there were a few. We just had to hope that one of them would be suitable.

The thrill of being back in Porto to actually view houses rather than just strolling round the city and dreaming did a lot to soothe our anxieties. We had arranged to view the only apartment on our list on our first full day in Porto. But the estate agent called shortly after breakfast to say that the apartment had been sold. Although it wasn't a good start to the week, in a way we were both a little relieved.

Perhaps unreasonably given our tight budget, we both really wanted a garden. And an apartment wouldn't be ideal for our cat Bibby, accustomed as he was to forty acres of wild hillside. We worried how he would cope with just a balcony, and even wondered if we could devise a basket and rope system to winch him down to street level each day. But we suspected he would consider such a system completely beneath his dignity.

As most of the houses we had arranged to view were in Vila Nova de Gaia, across the river from Porto, we had booked a hotel in Gaia. The hotel was modern and unremarkable but it was five minutes away from Coimbrões station. The station was badly signposted but we eventually stumbled across it at the end of a dusty cobbled lane dominated by a small abandoned factory and its huge brick chimney. We were becoming used to the way that urban areas in Portugal consist of an eclectic mix of many different types of buildings. Urban spaces seem more uniform in the UK; rows of terraced houses, vast housing estates, and industrial and retail parks. We liked the way that in Portugal tumbledown cottages, pristine modern apartments, and shops and cafes jostled cheek by jowl in a random but fascinating combination.

Waiting at the station for a train into Porto, I noticed an odd-looking single-storey house in a patch of waste ground. The house had a roof made of tin sheeting but its tiny front garden was a mass of flowers. A motley group of skinny cats slinked through the tangled greenery.

I nudged Geoff. 'I could live there.'

It was a game we had started to play on our first trip to Portugal, and it involved appraising all sorts of unlikely locations as possible future homes. So desperate were we to move that practically any dwelling, no matter how unsuitable, was declared ideal. In the first hotel we had stayed at, on Rua de Cedofeita, I frequently wandered onto the balcony, gazed down at the garden, and sighed, 'I could live here, in just this one room.'

On one of our previous train trips, we had seen an old tramp who was clearly spending his days riding the trains by dodging the ticket inspectors.

'Not a bad life, in a warm climate,' I had observed to Geoff. 'Given the choice, would you rather live in luxury in the UK or live on the trains here?'

'If it meant not going back to work, I'd live under a hedge,' he'd said firmly.

The only suitable house we had found in Porto was near Campanhã station and it was the first house that we viewed that week. It was also the most expensive on our list. In clear contravention of our insistence that we would be happy living just about anywhere, as long as it was in Portugal, we didn't like the Campanhã house. It had been completely renovated and tastefully decorated. It even had a good-sized garden. But it was on a busy road. The incessant traffic noise was the main thing that had driven us from our first home in Liverpool. The house was also very small. Downstairs, there was a living-cum-kitchen space and a bathroom. We didn't mind small; our cosy Welsh cottage was hardly spacious. But the one bedroom in the Campanhã house was essentially an attic; we climbed a very steep staircase to find ourselves under the eaves. And on the hot September day we visited, the bedroom was airless and stifling. We were thankful to escape back outside, and to take our leave of the disappointed estate agent, who tried his best to assure us that the owner would likely consider any offer we might care to make.

So that was Porto out. All our hopes were now pinned on the Vila Nova de Gaia viewings. On the morning of the viewings we stopped for breakfast at a characterful cafe not far from the train station. We had taken to frequenting this cafe for toast and coffee. The hotel's version of toasted bread was dry crispbread, which wasn't exactly a thrilling start to each day. The elderly owner of the cafe had eventually understood our garbled description in clumsy Portuguese and produced two servings of *torrada*, very thick bread toasted to perfection. He greeted us cheerily each morning and chattered away to us in Portuguese. We could only nod sagely and feel frustrated at our lack of proficiency.

We had decided, unwisely it turned out, to catch the train to Gaia centre and then walk to the estate agents. In Gaia, we tried to buy an ordnance survey map but were told that in Portugal only the military are allowed to possess such maps! As civilians, we were allowed only to buy a relatively simple area map. This we did, and armed with map and bottled water, set out to find the estate agents.

Gaia city centre is not large. The main commercial street, Avenida da República, is a pleasant wide boulevard lined with cafes and served by the Metro. Our route lay off this main thoroughfare and through a tangled maze of smaller streets and lanes. The day was hot and the map was infuriatingly vague. At one point, we found we had doubled back on ourselves and were nearly back where we had started.

Eventually we found ourselves in an attractive square shaded by tall plane trees. The road we needed was off this square somewhere. We were standing on a street corner poring over the map when we heard a gentle voice. We looked up to see a woman leaning out of the first-floor window of one of the houses looking onto the square. She had flung the shutters back and was resting her elbows on the windowsill, taking in the sun. She had seen our map and spotted our confusion and was obviously keen to help.

We told her the name of the road we were looking for and the name of the estate agents and by means of enthusiastic gestures, she managed to describe the correct route.

It turned out that we had been quite near our destination and soon found ourselves in the air-conditioned cool of the estate agent's office shaking hands with a stocky man with a disarming smile, who turned out to be Pedro Little Chicken. The mystery of Pedro's surname was solved when he introduced us to his colleague Cláudia, who spoke perfect English. She laughed uproariously when she learnt about the mistranslation.

'I told him to let me check the email before he sent it to you but no, he thinks he's a fluent English speaker now!'

Pedro could understand English better than he could speak it and he grinned sheepishly.

We had felt hot, flustered, and dishevelled after our long walk, but the informal friendliness of Pedro and Cláudia, and a welcome glass of mineral water, relaxed us and we were soon animatedly discussing the plan for the day with Pedro. We had assumed we would be heading straight off to view the properties we had enquired about but, we were told, things were not that simple. Two of the properties we were planning to view had been sold, Pedro told us apologetically. We asked about our favourite, the Riverside House. Perhaps we could go and view that first? Alas, we could not. The owners were away, but would be back later in the week. Our hearts sank. Out of a very small number of possibles, the Riverside House was the best option. We had come a long way to be told we couldn't see it.

But Pedro was cheerful. He promised to take us to see the Riverside House at the end of the week. In the meantime, he had taken the liberty of selecting some additional houses he knew we would be very interested in.

We weren't. As Pedro started to show us his selections

on the computer, we quickly sensed a theme. All the houses were expensive new builds, exactly the sort of place we didn't want. Pedro had obviously considerably overestimated our budget and underestimated our taste.

When we told him our meagre budget he shook his head sadly. 'I don't think we have many for that price,' he said.

When we explained to him that we were also looking for an older property, he looked astonished. He scrolled through the images on his computer and then showed us a picture of a grey modern house that looked, we thought, like a concrete box.

'You don't like this?'

We shook our heads.

He scrolled again and showed us an image of a ruined old manor house. 'You like this better?'

'Well, perhaps a bit less of a ruin, but yes, we prefer that type of house.'

He gave us the kind of look that people reserve for the very young, very old, or very insane and smiled patiently. 'I see what I can do.'

After a hurried conflab with Cláudia, more frantic scrolling on the computer, and several phone calls, Pedro announced that he had found some houses he knew would be perfect for us. We swallowed our reservations and got in the car with him and Cláudia.

All that afternoon and the following day we were treated to an exhausting but memorable tour of a bewildering array of houses in various states of decay. Pedro drove at a snail's pace through the narrow picturesque lanes of Gaia, with Cláudia constantly cracking jokes about his driving and reeling off a fascinating array of information about each area we visited.

I will not recount here all the houses we visited, but they provided an eye-opening introduction to older Portuguese real estate in all its shabby glory. While not exactly ruins, some of the houses we viewed that week were in a shocking state of disrepair. In Portugal, a combination of inheritance laws and climate (baking hot summers and occasional torrential rain) means that older houses often degenerate surprisingly quickly. For example, we were taken to see one house in what we were told was quite an upmarket area of Gaia. The house was tidy and detached and from the street seemed perfectly pleasant. However, the back view of the house revealed a bowing roof line and huge cracks down the outer wall — a clear sign of subsidence. Despite this, the price was at the very top of our budget.

Pedro and Cláudia assumed that we wanted to be as close to the city centre as possible, and seemed surprised when we revealed that we were happy to look at properties a little further afield. We had quickly realized that you didn't get a lot for your money in central Gaia.

For example, we went to see one house in the riverside quarter. The house was well-proportioned and on a pretty cobbled street. As we went through the tidy front gate, we were greeted by a friendly middle-aged woman, who we assumed was the owner. We were shown up a flight of external stairs to the first floor. Inside, the rooms were spacious and had been newly decorated. The house had a stunning view of the river and a large back garden.

'Could we ask the owner one or two things about the garden?' I said to Cláudia.

'Oh, she isn't here,' Cláudia said. 'We can phone her and ask.'

'But wasn't that her at the gate?'

'Oh no,' Cláudia said. 'That woman just lives downstairs.'

I had read several far-fetched horror stories on the Internet about expats buying houses abroad and then discovering a clause in the deeds that allows Great Uncle So and So to live in the house for perpetuity.

'You mean, she won't move out?' I asked Cláudia.

'No no,' she laughed. 'This house ... it's an *andar moradia.*'

We looked blank.

'It means there are two houses in the same building. The ground floor is one house, and the upper floor is another house.'

Light dawned. It became clear why we had been shown straight to the upper floor. This attractive property was actually within our budget and we now knew why. It was half a house that was for sale.

We confessed to Pedro and Cláudia that we had been hoping to buy a whole house and preferably one with a garden, even if it meant being further away from the city centre. Despite our initial conviction that we could make do with practically any dwelling if it meant being in Portugal, our tour of the Gaia properties had prompted a yearning for some outside space. We had been growing as much of our own food as we could for the last thirteen years. It would be hard to adapt to life without a garden.

Before taking us further afield, Cláudia insisted we see one last city centre property. It had a garden that was *fantástico* she explained. The house, apparently, was less impressive, but she thought we should see it.

We pulled up in a quiet residential street near Santo Silva Hospital. Between two very modern properties was a large plot of land. Through the leaves of numerous fruit trees we glimpsed a dwelling. This was more like it.

Cláudia pushed open the rickety front gate and then turned and looked at us solemnly. 'This one,' she said, 'is ... um ... how do you say in English ... a bit of a ghetto.'

We laughed. 'I don't think that's the word you want,' Geoff said. 'A ghetto is like a slum dwelling, you know, a shack or something.'

Cláudia gazed towards the house thoughtfully. 'No,' she said, 'ghetto is the right word. Look.'

The house we were standing in front of was of one storey and about the size of a large garden shed. It had two rooms, according to Cláudia, but we couldn't see them because it was too dangerous to actually enter the house. We had worked this out for ourselves because where part of the roof should have been, the top branches of a vigorous looking fig tree swayed in the breeze.

'See what I mean?' Cláudia said. 'A ghetto. But you can pull it down, start again. Build a nice big house and a swimming pool.'

We didn't want a nice big house and a swimming pool; we wanted somewhere small and manageable with a decent garden. This place certainly had the garden, and if the house had been at all liveable we would have been very tempted. But the prospect of planning applications and a major building project was a big turn-off. We reluctantly tore ourselves away from that wonderful garden and headed back to the car.

We were soon down to the last two houses on Pedro and Cláudia's list. We went first to a house situated down a quiet cobbled lane. Pedro led us through wrought iron gates into an attractive courtyard. This looked promising. However, we were bewildered to find a small group of people waiting for us in the courtyard. They greeted us warmly and asked our names. The reason for their interest soon became apparent. The courtyard was actually a communal space and was bordered by four different dwellings, only one of which was up for sale. It was essential a small hamlet; if we bought the available house the two of us would make up a quarter of the hamlet's residents. Cosy. A bit too cosy for our tastes.

There was no doubt, however, of the welcoming nature of our would-be neighbours. One of them was particularly friendly and accompanied us as we followed Pedro around the property. Through Pedro, she explained that she lived next door and that once we had moved in, we must not hesitate to call on her for any help we might need. She pointed out features of the house she thought we might like, including a large persimmon tree in the back garden. The house was solid and roomy and our new friend so charming that we were almost tempted to put in an offer. But we had the sense to realize that for two chronic introverts like ourselves, being adopted by this tiny community, though nice in one way, would prove difficult.

As we took our leave, the courtyard inhabitants were setting up a small outdoor grill and opening bottles of wine. We took our leave somewhat guiltily, refusing their offer to join them. Pedro looked a little disappointed we weren't staying for supper, but then began eyeing the gate nervously when one of the courtyard dogs, a rather belligerent looking sheepdog, seemed to take a shine to him. As we headed for the gate, Pedro was bringing up the rear. Myself, Geoff, and Cláudia slipped out and Geoff gently closed the gate on Pedro, smiling mischievously at Cláudia and myself.

If there had been a cup for athletic prowess in estate agents, Pedro would have won it, as he practically sprinted the last few yards. He clung on to the gate, smiling nervously and sweating profusely as the courtyard dogs, sensing sport, tailed him. Their owners followed, shouting reassurance. The sight reduced Cláudia to helpless laughter and she clutched me, trying to catch her breath, as Geoff waited until the last moment to swing open the gate to let poor Pedro out. By the time we had reached the car, Pedro had recovered his usual ebullience and was insisting that he hadn't been in the least bit worried about the dogs.

The last house we went to see was the only real competitor to the Riverside House. It was a tall square house in the middle of a good-sized plot. We liked the garden, which had a pretty vegetable plot and a little shed. The house had a kitchen that was straight out of the 1950s but the sitting room was large and there was a sunny study that looked out over the garden. Curiously, a large portion of the space was taken up by an elaborate regal staircase that opened onto an enormous landing which ran round the entire upper floor. Unfortunately, this meant that the four bedrooms and two bathrooms were all tiny. Without some structural work, we couldn't see the house working for us. And at eighty thousand euros, it was at the very top of our budget. That left nothing for any renovations. However, it was the best we had seen. And until we could see the elusive Riverside House, it was the only contender. We were beginning to fear that finding our dream house in Portugal might remain just a dream.

5

Viewing houses didn't leave much time for more leisurely activities, but we tried that week to fit in some time exploring Porto. For both of us, this was more an attempt to reassure ourselves that we had chosen the right place to live, rather than a desire for sightseeing. We hadn't lived full-time in a big city for ten years; would we really be happy living in Porto?

One day, we took an open-top bus tour to try to familiarize ourselves with those areas of the city we hadn't previously explored on foot. From the top floor of the bus, we gazed down onto pavement cafes and into the upper storey windows of traditional town houses, their window-boxes bright with flowers. We admired the smart apartments and mansions lining Avenida da Boavista and marvelled as the avenue unexpectedly reached the sea and the urban landscape was replaced with empty beaches and the scent of salt air. As the bus wound its way through the port of Matosinhos, we drank in the sights, sounds, and smells of the bustling fish restaurants lining the coastal strip until we were soon speeding under the shade of large trees as the bus followed the road upriver to the Ribeira quarter.

It was a whirlwind tour, but it confirmed our conviction

that we had chosen our future home well. Porto seemed to have most of the qualities we could have wished for. It had history, beauty, and the bustle of a large city, but also quiet squares and leafy avenues. What was more, it had access to both the river and the sea. For ten years, we had lived in the hills of Snowdonia, and grown familiar with mountain air and green vistas. Perhaps it was time for a change. Perhaps it was time to get to know the moods of a river and to feel the energy of the sea.

The day before we were due to fly home, Pedro called to announce he had arranged a viewing of the Riverside House. At last! We had pored over the estate agent's photographs of the house for weeks, checking the website obsessively to make sure that the house hadn't been sold. Even from the photos, the house felt right. We hoped that our instincts weren't wrong and that we hadn't fallen in love with another of Cláudia's 'ghettos'.

We needn't have worried. The house was in a parish that was not very far from Gaia city centre, but seemed a world away. We drove with Pedro and Cláudia through steep winding lanes, many of them cobbled. As we drove, we caught glimpses of the river between the houses. Suddenly Pedro pulled into a spot where the road widened. We got out and stared open-mouthed at the view. Although not far from the river, we were at quite an elevation.

The lane we were on curved round in a horseshoe shape. It was bordered by a handful of houses, all different, and on this hot afternoon it was very quiet. At the top of the horseshoe, the vista opened up to reveal the blue expanse of the River Douro. This was more than we could have hoped for. I prayed that the house we were about to view wasn't just a glorified shed because it would be hard to walk away from that view.

A short stroll down the lane was what looked like a single-storey dwelling. We were a little disappointed to see that there were three front doors: it was a terraced house after all, and a very small one at that. But Pedro was at pains to correct us and insisted that the house was definitely 'four fronts'. The meaning of this mysterious expression soon became clear when he led us round the side of the house. 'Four fronts' meant that the house was in fact detached. It just had two front doors too many. However, when Pedro unlocked one of the doors and led us through, we found ourselves, not inside the house, but on a small flight of steps that led down to a small secluded garden. To the right of the steps was a patio on which stood a stone outbuilding, the outside wall of which bordered the lane. We liked the space immediately; we had long been charmed by the design of Moorish houses with their simple high streetside walls that conceal cool intimate courtyards.

We followed Pedro down the steps and glanced at the garden as he unlocked the door. The space wasn't large but it was bright with tidy flowerbeds and shaded by an orange tree. So far, so good, we thought. But the structure we were shown into didn't look very promising. The roof was corrugated plastic and worn tiles lined the walls. However, this turned out to be a kind of porch and led into a decent-sized kitchen. The decor was very dated: the wall cupboards were pure 1950s and the large sink was of stone. But we loved the Escher-like black and white floor tiles and the little skylight. Like the kitchen in our Welsh cottage, this kitchen was half underground and the sill of the little window over the sink was at ground level and looked out onto a pot full of flowers. It was a good sign.

The kitchen gave onto a small dining room, which was dominated by an enormous wardrobe. Pedro explained that the room had been used as a bedroom in the past. Narrow glazed wooden French double doors opened from the dining room into a large sitting room. We liked the light and space in this room, which had two large double windows. One faced south and looked out onto the small garden with the orange tree. The other window faced east and after some struggling with the old-fashioned catch, Cláudia managed to open it wide.

'Come and look,' she said.

We went to the window and leaned on the stone sill. We were looking out over the back of the house and because of the slope of the hill, this window was at first-floor level. To our delight, the garden was bigger than we had thought; from our vantage point, we could see a flight of steps that led down enticingly to another garden space. But it was the river that captured our gaze. Broad and calm, the water seemed to glitter in the strong light. We could just make out a small beach on the other side of the river and the tiny figures of sunbathers. This was as different as you could get from our damp green Welsh hillside and the dull inner-city setting of our Liverpool house. Was it possible that we had found a real gem in this old riverside house?

Unfortunately, a tour of the upper floor revealed some of the flaws in this gem of a house. The ceilings of the three bedrooms were adorned with elaborate wooden chandeliers, but in the largest bedroom the ceiling had partly collapsed, a sure sign of a dodgy roof. Great. The bathroom was a decent size, with a large bath. However, tell-tale rust streaks on the enamel suggested that the plumbing wasn't in great shape either. An unusual feature of the house was that it had two staircases. The second staircase led from one of the bedrooms to the dining room and was so rotten that it was coming away from the wall. More work, then.

But there were aspects of this house that we knew we could fall in love with. Two of the bedrooms had original full-length wooden shutters and pretty stained glass panels above the internal doors. We liked the quirky split-level garden and the old terrazzo tiles in the little porch. And there was that view again. The smallest bedroom was at the back of the house and we flung open the casement windows to gaze out. The fronds of a palm tree in the garden of the house across the way moved gently in the river breeze. We breathed in the clear warm air and were smitten.

The little garden had distinct possibilities ... and a few surprises. Half-hidden among the weeds, we found an iron wheel with a handle on it that we took to be ornamental. However, it was nothing of the sort. It seemed that the house had a well that was the sole water supply. Pedro pointed to a rusting tank on the kitchen roof. Water was gravity fed from this tank to the house, but the tank had to be filled at intervals by manually turning the well wheel. We might have been near Portugal's second largest city, but this set-up was not so different to that of our Welsh cottage in the mountains!

In the corner of the garden near the well was a large stone tank with a sloping top which we quizzed Cláudia about.

'It's for washing clothes,' she explained. 'You press the clothes here to wring them out, and the stone slopes to drain off the water.'

This was one feature our Welsh cottage didn't have. But then, doing laundry outside in a roaring Welsh gale was not a popular pastime in Snowdonia.

A thought occurred to me. 'Cláudia, what did Pedro mean when he said in his email that this house was next to a washing machine?'

Cláudia guffawed. She shouted something in Portuguese to Pedro, who was poking around in the lower garden. He laughed and shook his head in mock despair.

'I'll show you what he meant,' she said. 'You don't have

to use this little tank to wash your clothes at all. Follow me.'

This sounded promising. Maybe there was an outhouse with a washing machine, we thought.

But no. Cláudia led us across the garden to a small terrace and pointed down at a large stone structure not far from the house.

'What is it?'

'It's the local *lavadouro*,' Cláudia explained.

'The what?'

'*Lavadouro* ... the wash-house. It's like your tank over there, but much bigger. In Portugal, we have lots of them. This one is very old but I think many people still use it.'

And indeed, as we gazed down we could hear voices and the sound of splashing.

'See?' Cláudia said. 'You can wash your clothes down there!'

Spending the day at a public wash-house, no matter how traditional, wasn't exactly my idea of the perfect Iberian pastime but at least, I supposed, we would have the weather for it.

On the way back to the car, my phone rang. It was our estate agent to say that we had had a good offer on the Halfway House. It couldn't have come at a better time. On the way back to the office we stopped at a cafe for coffee. Pedro and Cláudia produced a sheaf of forms to note down our impressions of the various houses we had viewed.

'What is your favourite house?' Cláudia asked.

'The last one, the one by the river,' Geoff said. He looked at me. 'In fact, I think we want to make an offer, don't we?'

I nodded.

Pedro and Cláudia were jubilant. Astonished by our penchant for old rundown properties, I think that until that moment they had doubted we might actually go through with buying a house in Portugal. But the Riverside House was exactly what we were looking for, and at sixty thousand euros it was well within budget. However, it needed work, a lot of work. Cláudia promised to arrange some quotes from local builders and, reluctantly, we prepared to fly back to the UK.

That last evening in Portugal was a bit like a dream. We had managed, against expectations, to find a characterful little house in a stunning location that we could actually afford. There was a lot of work ahead but it looked like our dream of living in Portugal might actually be realized. Over a celebratory dinner, we gazed at the photographs we had taken of the Riverside House and excitedly discussed our plans.

Strolling back to the hotel after dinner, we took a wrong turn down a little lane and suddenly found ourselves in the middle of a small crowd of people. There seemed to be some kind of party going on; there was lots of laughter and glasses of wine were being passed around. The group were gathered around what turned out to be a small stage. Hemmed in by partygoers we stood and watched as a group of musicians took to the stage and started tuning their instruments.

Reluctant to wait for the music, an elderly man next to us starting jigging on the spot, smiling broadly and encouraging us to join him. Embarrassed at stumbling into a private festa, we tried to edge our way back to the main road. The little group obviously knew that we were strangers but seemed quite happy for us to join them; one woman tried to press glasses of wine into our hands and pointed to a barbecue, concerned that we might leave hungry. The little episode seemed a good omen and a perfect end to a life-changing week. In the light of subsequent events, we looked back on that warm happy evening as the lull before the storm.

Back in the UK, reality hit home. Although we had accepted an offer on the Halfway House, there were still a few viewings that we had to honour and we still had some possessions to try and sell before we moved. We lived in constant worry that someone else would buy the Riverside House before our own house sale went through, but we could do little but sit tight and hope.

At least one worry had proved foundless. We had been concerned about the effect of our next door neighbours the NeoClampetts on any prospective buyers. Would one of their frequent deafening family arguments erupt while we were showing people round? Happily, it turned out that the people who were keen to buy the Halfway House already knew the NeoClampetts, having been cursed with the bad luck of having them as neighbours some years ago. They grinned at us knowingly when they told us, and seemed sanguine at being saddled with them again.

Never having moved countries before, there seemed an endless list of arrangements to be made. We discussed customs regulations with removal firms, applied for a pet passport for Bibby, and found an apartment to rent in Gaia while the building work on our new home was carried out.

We also found ourselves an English-speaking lawyer to manage the purchase of the Riverside House. We found Henrique on a Portuguese website and he wrote us long and thoughtful emails in fluent English. He warned us against signing any documents before he had seen them, and generally tried to persuade us of the malevolent and unscrupulous nature of all estate agents. He urged us to try and remember if we had inadvertently signed anything while we had been house-hunting with Pedro and Cláudia, and clearly didn't believe us when we insisted that no, we hadn't been pressured into buying a ruined *quinta* with three hundred acres.

We decided to arrange a brief visit to Porto to meet up with Henrique, sign the house purchase documents, and see the building estimates that Cláudia had obtained for us. The sale of the Halfway House had proceeded surprisingly quickly and we now had a moving date, but we reasoned that it would be useful to finalize things at the Portugal end before the actual move. And we needed little excuse for another quick trip to our adopted country. So we flew to Porto with light hearts, eager to begin the transition to a new life. And disaster struck.

We had found our way to the *câmara*, the council building where we were to meet up with Henrique and the couple selling the Riverside House to complete the necessary paperwork. In Portugal, this process is quite formal. All papers are signed in the presence of lawyers for both the seller and the buyer and in the presence of council officials, who oversee the whole process and talk everyone through the details of each document.

We had met up with Henrique for the first time the previous day, although he had been over an hour late for our appointment. Dapper and urbane, Henrique was charming and helpful and provided a running commentary on all aspects of life in Portugal. He was a fascinating character but, we were to learn, his timekeeping was appalling. On the morning we were due to sign the papers at the *câmara*, Henrique phoned to say that he had been briefly delayed. We all stood in the foyer, stiff and overdressed, for almost an hour until Henrique came flying in the door, all crumpled jacket and humble apologies.

Afterwards, we couldn't resist a brief visit to the Riverside House. The day was hot, and we took the bus and plodded up the steep hill to our lane. We wandered around the house and garden wonderingly, still unable to believe that it was ours. We were sitting on the back step admiring the orange tree when Geoff had an odd sensation. The vision in his right eye changed. He experienced bright flashes of light not related to any external stimuli. When he tried to focus on anything with that eye, the vision became blurred. Worried, we caught the bus back to the hotel, hoping that it was just the heat.

But it wasn't. The next morning, Geoff's eye was no better. We were due to fly home in the late afternoon so we travelled into Gaia centre and found an opticians shop. The optician told us to go straight to the local hospital.

The eye department at the hospital was very accommodating and gave Geoff a thorough examination. He was told that his symptoms indicated a problem with the optic nerve, but that it may well resolve naturally. Learning that we were due to move to Portugal, the doctor asked Geoff to come back to the hospital if his vision didn't clear up.

We flew back to the UK and hoped for the best. But a day later, we found ourselves in the emergency department of a hospital in Liverpool. Geoff's vision had worsened. The doctor there confirmed that the problem was with the optic nerve, but did not think that it was likely to improve. And he was puzzled about the cause of the problem.

'Have you had any illnesses in the last few months?'

'I had a bad flu-type thing a couple of months ago.'

In fact, we had both had an odd sort of flu that had some strange symptoms. And we had read that some viruses can cause eye problems.

But the doctor seemed to have a different focus. 'Your blood pressure is very high,' he commented

'It always is around doctors,' Geoff said. 'It's normal at home.'

'Hmmm. Are you taking any medication for it?'

'No. Like I said, it's absolutely normal when I'm at home. I just get stressed when I'm around doctors. I think it's called "white coat hypertension" isn't it?'

'I think your high blood pressure caused your eye problem.'

'But I don't have high blood pressure!'

'It's high now.'

'Only because I'm talking to you!'

And so it went on. Once the doctors had convinced themselves that Geoff had a blood pressure problem, they stopped looking for any other explanation for what he had experienced with his eye. They sent him home with a prescription for hypertensives and that was that. With only two weeks to our moving date, we had to make some hard decisions.

'Maybe we should stay in the UK,' I said. 'You can do without the stress of a move right now.'

But Geoff was adamant. 'I want to move,' he insisted. 'I won't feel any better about this if we stay here. In fact, it would make me feel worse.'

There was another reason why we pressed on with the move. We couldn't afford not to. We were now both out of work and reluctant to apply for jobs at other universities. We were done with academia. Property was much more expensive in the UK than in Portugal, and we couldn't afford to buy a house in the city outright. And our redundancy payments wouldn't last long if we stayed at the Halfway House and continued to pay the mortgage. Portugal was, it seemed, our best option.

I remember those last two weeks in the UK as an unhappy blur of activities — last-minute packing, goodbyes to family and friends — that would have been rather exciting in normal circumstances but were now overlaid with an aura of worry and dismay. But finally, we were on a one-way flight to Porto, trailing what seemed like a lot of burnt bridges and unsure of what our future might hold.

6

Those first few weeks in Portugal were strange for several reasons. Life had seemed rather unreal since the episode with Geoff's eye. We felt disoriented, our plans no longer so certain. But we had a house to renovate and a new life to build. We had coped with hardships (of a different kind) in our years at the cottage and had learnt that sometimes you had to just get on with life and trust that things would work out.

Living in the wilderness in Wales had also taught us to be self-reliant. Hoping to find some answers, Geoff had returned to the doctor at the eye hospital who provided pretty much the same diagnosis as the doctor in Liverpool and took Geoff's blood pressure, which of course had skyrocketed as soon as we had arrived at the hospital. Clutching yet another prescription for antihypertensives, we gave up and left.

'I'll just have to figure things out for myself,' Geoff said. 'Blood pressure medication isn't the answer.'

It didn't help that we were between homes. We had arranged a three-month lease on an apartment within striking distance of the Riverside House. Although we had originally intended living in our new home while the renovation work was being carried out, a glance at the list of essential building work had put paid to that idea. We needed somewhere clean and quiet to stay while ceilings were being dismantled and floorboards taken up.

The apartment was in a quiet neighbourhood on the hill of Monte da Virgem, in Gaia. The hill is home to a huge mast owned by RTP, the Portuguese equivalent of the BBC. Because of its altitude, the mast can be seen from any area in Gaia and Pedro and Cláudia had advised us that if we ever needed to find our bearings, we need only look for its distinctive shape on the skyline.

From Monte da Virgem, the land slopes down to the seaside parish of Canidelo, with its smart apartments and restaurants. On one of the apartment's two balconies, we could see the sea sparkling in the distance and marvel at the jumble of red tiled roofs and lush gardens.

The apartment itself was light and spacious. In fact, it was bigger than we needed but our choice of rentals had been restricted because we needed somewhere that was pet-friendly. Sofia, our landlady, confessed that she was crazy about cats and was eager to meet Bibby, who was experiencing his first continental tour. Rather than submit him to a plane journey, we had arranged with a pet courier for him to be driven overland to Portugal via France and Spain. He arrived in Porto three days after we did and seemed none the worse for his journey, although he was a little wild-eyed and would barely look at us for an hour or two.

Most of our belongings were in storage and with little to do, life was slower than it had been for months. Tired after the stress of the move, we read, shopped for groceries at the tiny *mini-mercado* nearby, and stood on the apartment balcony staring at the sea. Sometimes we wandered out into the quiet streets near the apartment to look for interesting cafes.

We had discovered that one of the small pleasures of living in Portugal is the plethora of independent coffee shops. Even in quiet residential areas, there seems to be one every few yards. And they were a revelation. In the UK, we had often felt that a trip to a cafe was a hit or miss affair. We had sometimes chanced on little places that managed to offer an imaginative range of homemade food and delicious fresh coffee. Other times we had grumbled over shrink-wrapped sandwiches and weak lukewarm tea. In Portugal, it seemed that you could eat well in almost every cafe you stumbled across.

The little place on a quiet corner near our apartment, which quickly became our 'local', was a good example. An unassuming frontage concealed a dimly lit interior filled with interesting features that seemed more suited to a grander establishment. The tables and chairs were of decorative polished wood. Pretty blue and yellow tiles ran round the bottom half of the walls; above these, a row of brass-framed mirrors reflected the shelves behind the counter, which were filled with glasses, bottles of all kinds of liquor, and potted plants. A huge gleaming espresso machine was the sole modern touch.

The cafe seemed to have little passing trade but it served a wide range of food and drink. You could opt for just a freshly made pastry or cake, maybe one of the deliciously creamy *pasteis de nata*. Or you could choose from several different types of *lanche*, a puff pastry savoury filled with ham and cheese, chicken, or spinach. If you were hungrier you could opt for soup, or perhaps ask what the dish of the day was, maybe freshly caught bream with potatoes and other vegetables.

It was no easier deciding what to drink. There were many different types of coffee on offer, a range of teas, and freshly squeezed orange juice. Or perhaps (because

Portuguese cafes are licensed) you would prefer a cold glass of beer, like a Sagres (brewed in the south of Portugal) or a Superbock (brewed in the north), a glass of regional wine, or a brandy.

To save money, we usually ate meals at the apartment and then slipped out for coffee and cake. The little cafe was often empty and we would take a book and linger at our table near the window, or sit outside and take in the sun. Although it was autumn, the weather was warm and sunny and we marvelled at the novelty of sitting outside in tee-shirts in October.

Twice a week, we took a bus journey to visit the house and to remind ourselves that yes, we had done it, we had actually bought a house in Portugal. We had secured the services of Jorge, a local builder who had provided a quote for the rather extensive renovation work that the house needed. Short but stocky, with a ready laugh and an energetic manner, Jorge seemed the man for the job. At least, we thought he was, based on our limited ability to communicate with the man.

Our first real meeting with Jorge took place at the estate agents. Cláudia explained that Jorge wanted to talk us through the planned work on the house and check some details with us and had proposed we drive out to the house together. Unfortunately, she could not accompany us that day.

'But you'll be okay!' she smiled encouragingly. 'You can speak some Portuguese and Jorge can speak a little bit of English. It will be fun!'

We doubted it. Our pidgin Portuguese didn't extend to builder-speak or the plethora of technical terms involved in a large-scale renovation. And Jorge's English vocabulary wouldn't get us very far. Bouncing around in his battered white truck as it clattered over the cobbled streets, we listened as he proudly recited the four English words he knew: ‘yes’, ‘no’, ‘hello,’ and (for some reason we were never able to fathom) ‘cauliflower’. It was going to be a long morning.

However, it seemed that Jorge was in no hurry to get to the house. First, we stopped at a small cafe round the corner from the estate agents. Jorge ordered three *cafezinhos*, one-shot espressos. He knocked his back in one mouthful then looked expectantly at us. We hurriedly sipped the scalding hot coffee and then we were off again in the truck. Our second stop was a florist’s shop to pick up Jorge’s wife, who worked there. We dropped her off in front of a block of apartments and then were off again, but apparently not to the house.

Jorge headed instead for the maze of narrow streets near to the Cais de Gaia, the riverfront. He pulled up outside a tall townhouse and rang the bell. Mystified, we allowed ourselves to be ushered inside. Over tea and biscuits, it became clear why we were there. Our host was Marianne, a Dutch lady who explained that she and her husband had bought the house a year ago and commissioned Jorge and his team for the renovation. Jorge was obviously eager to showcase his skills and we were treated to an extensive tour of the house and a rather detailed explanation of the work, expertly translated for us by Marianne, whose Portuguese language skills were, we noted enviously, a hell of a lot better than ours.

Finally, Jorge drove us to our own house, which looked particularly shabby after seeing Marianne’s. Armed with his copy of the renovation jobs we had agreed to, Jorge raced round every inch of the house and garden like a small tornado, firing questions at us that we didn’t understand. As we had some experience in house renovation, we were able to guess at some of his queries but others were impenetrable. For example, one of his frequent questions was what sounded like '*leeshoo*?' uttered while pointing at various things, such as the stone wash tank in the garden and the floorboards in the bedroom.

We were perplexed. What was this mysterious *leeshoo*? Jorge found a bit of paper and wrote the word down for us: it was in fact spelt *lixo*. But we were none the wiser. We stared hard at the word as if knowing its correct spelling would magically reveal its meaning. It didn't. Jorge seemed to want a yes or no answer, but we were reluctant to say '*sim*' or '*não*' without knowing what we were agreeing to. The mistake could prove expensive. So we could only respond to his earnest queries with apologetic shrugs.

Finally, Jorge hit upon the idea of using mime. He grabbed some old sacks that were lying in the lower garden and threw them into a corner, shouting 'Lixo!'

He looked at us expectantly and we stared at the sacks hopefully. Jorge picked up two cracked plastic flowerpots and threw them on top of the sacks.

'Maybe he's building a bonfire,' I said.

Jorge cast about, rather desperately I thought, for something else for his mime. He lighted on the attractive wrought iron gate set into the garden wall.

'Não lixo!' he announced emphatically. We followed his gaze from the gate to the pile of sacks and old pots and back again.

'I've got it,' Geoff shouted. 'It's rubbish!'

'What is?'

'Lixo. It means rubbish!'

'So that's what he was asking us!'

I'm not exaggerating when I say that it felt like a revelation to have figured this out. Unfortunately, it meant that we had to repeat our tour of the house and garden pointing out to Jorge exactly what we wanted to keep and what was *lixo*. It was good that we did; some of the original features that we most admired, such as the old wooden floorboards in the bedroom and the worn but beautiful terrazzo floor tiles in the bathroom, Jorge was keen to replace and had to be convinced that, where possible, we wanted him to *reparar* rather than to *destruir*.

Despite our conservative approach, the amount of stuff in the *lixo* category seemed to be growing. To the dodgy staircase, the cracked wall tiles, and the acres of chicken wire in the lower garden, we reluctantly added the nice 1950s kitchen cupboards, which turned out on closer inspection to be rotten, and the stone kitchen sink, which Jorge pointed out was cracked.

Then there was the large stone outbuilding. Romantically draped with wisteria and with views of the river, we had originally imagined this as a perfect little writing den, a place to dream away the days. However, removal of the vegetation revealed that the outbuilding's stone walls were leaning dangerously and that part of the roof had fallen in. As our budget wouldn't stretch to restoring romantic ruins, especially ones that were dangerously derelict, we agreed with Jorge that the building should be taken down and replaced with an open-sided structure.

We also raised with him the idea of installing solar panels on our roof. It had occurred to us that we should make the most of the sunnier climate by having a small solar array. At our cottage in Wales, we had depended upon solar power for all our electricity and even though the Riverside House was connected to mains electricity, it would be a shame to be completely 'on grid'. The garden, and our budget, weren't big enough to install a large system but we had the space for about four solar panels, which would give us a reasonable amount of power. Geoff drew a diagram for Jorge to explain what we wanted and he promised he would find someone to install the panels.

The eventual list of renovations we agreed with Jorge was alarmingly long and included replacing the ceilings, replastering, replumbing, rewiring, fixing up the tiled roof as much as possible (we couldn't afford to completely replace it), and re-rendering and painting the outside walls. There was little we could do except let Jorge and his team get on and soon the place was swarming with a motley group of workmen which seemed to constantly change according to the task in hand.

However, we grew to recognize two of Jorge's regular workmen: a tanned wiry character who we were sure could probably break the Olympic record for speed tiling, and a huge lumbering chap whose specialty seemed to be hitting things and who we found one day demolishing one of the outbuilding walls practically single handed.

In between visits to the house, we explored the shops in Porto and Gaia searching for household linens, crockery, and other essentials. We had brought so little with us we needed practically everything. We bought excellent quality bedding from the textile shops in Porto, cups and plates from the open-air markets, and a kettle and toaster from El Corte Inglés, a huge old-style department store on Gaia's Avenida da República. The store's plush interior and lavish window displays evoke the atmosphere of the grand British department stores of the past.

We stored our purchases in Sofia's apartment, where they were a welcome reminder that soon we would have our own place. Until then, we felt in limbo; we had successfully moved to Portugal but it was impossible to really settle in as we were between homes.

Bibby also seemed weary of apartment living. Despite its sea view, he was not impressed by the apartment balcony. To add insult to injury, he was only allowed out there on his little lead. The balcony was enclosed by wrought iron, which afforded multiple gaps for Bibby, a notoriously clumsy cat, to fall or jump through.

He got his revenge on us by spending the day padding through the apartment from room to room and systematically lying on every single piece of furniture. The apartment was large, and had four bedrooms and multiple sofas and chairs. We were horrified when we realized that Bibby was managing to leave a trail of cat hairs on every bed and sofa in the place. Our attempts to keep all doors closed at all times were fruitless, as Bibby had worked out how to swing on the handles and let himself through.

We eventually bought some cheap bed sheets and laid these on the soft furnishings. When Sofia called round one day, she looked curiously at the draped furniture and pointed out that there was spare bed linen in one of the cupboards if we needed it. When we confessed to Bibby's crime, she burst into laughter and scooped him up in her arms. On their first meeting, she had been smitten with our cat and now, apparently, he could do no wrong.

'Let him lie where he wants,' she said, tenderly feeding Bibby the expensive cat treats she had brought with her. 'He doesn't mean any harm.'

We glared at Bibby disbelievingly and said nothing. Despite her protestations, we knew that Sofia wouldn't appreciate having to steam clean all the furnishings after we had left, so the bedsheets stayed put.

Although the major building work on the house was finished just before Christmas, Jorge still had to install the new kitchen and bathroom and finish the painting and decorating. We resigned ourselves to Christmas and New Year in the apartment. The big windows and high ceilings that made the apartment sunny and airy in summer ensured that it was cold and damp in winter. We huddled round a calor gas heater with a grumpy Bibby to toast the end of the year with glasses of port and slices of *bolo rei*, the traditional fruit cake eaten at *Natal*.

The day before, we had ventured into Porto to admire the festive lights but the grey skies and the chilly streets had hastened us back to the apartment. It was hardly the Christmas in the sun we had envisaged. Still, we would soon be in our new home. We could only hope that the coming year would prove less stressful than the last one.

7

With the midwinter solstice behind us, we felt a sense of relief. Jorge had promised that the house would be ready by the end of January, so we could now turn our attention to hunting for furniture, rugs, and lighting. But first we needed a kitchen. Jorge suggested a trip to Ikea to check out their fitted kitchens. While we were there, we could look at furniture and appliances.

In the UK, we had rather naively imagined ourselves strolling round Porto's antique shops and markets, choosing unusual old pieces for our new home. However, a general lack of money, time, and independent transport meant that this daydream wasn't going to materialize. We readily agreed to Jorge's proposal and so one cold morning in January, we got up early and made our way to the corner of the lane where Jorge had arranged to pick us up.

Although there was a chill in the air, the blazing sunshine reminded us that we were in Portugal, and prompted the slight feeling of unreality we both still experienced sometimes. It takes time to settle into a new country. It is as if one's physical and mental rhythms have to adjust to a new climate, a different atmosphere, a foreign spirit. In those early months, we felt between worlds, rootless and in a kind of limbo.

Jorge turned up on time and full of beans as usual. We climbed into the back seat of his truck and exchanged *Bom dias* with his wife, who had insisted on coming along. A visit to Ikea was obviously a rare treat. As we sped along the motorway, we struggled to keep up with Jorge's chatter, catching only the odd word now and again.

Jorge had brought the kitchen measurements with him and before the end of the day, we had managed to purchase a kitchen and most of the furniture we needed and load it into the truck. Before we left, we went to check out the appliances. Geoff and I headed for the washing machines but Jorge steered us towards what he obviously considered more important: *máquinas de lavar loiça*, dishwashers.

'Oh no, we don't need one of those,' I shook my head. '*Nao queremos*.'

Neither of us were big fans of dishwashers; we had never really felt the need for one. Jorge looked at us wide-eyed, incredulous at our lack of interest.

'Não quiser?' he asked.

We shook our heads. Jorge's wife took my arm and launched into a rather impassioned speech that we could only assume was about the desirability of owning one of these marvellous labour-saving devices. When I smiled and shook my head, she looked at me regretfully, obviously concluding that I had just committed myself to a life of servitude at the kitchen sink.

Later, we reflected on the curious popularity of the dishwasher in Portugal. In Ikea and other stores we had visited, we had noticed that the range of dishwashers on sale was far larger than that of washing machines. In Sofia's apartment, the large dishwasher took pride of place in the kitchen, while the small, rather ancient washing machine was relegated to the *marquise*, a kind of large balcony enclosed by glass panels. We had noticed that many apartments and houses, including our own, had *marquises*, which were used for hanging out laundry (the tumble dryer is not a popular appliance in Portugal).

Then something clicked. Our friends in Wales, Sal and Sam, had had a huge dishwasher and used it with gusto. They often commented on how the machine was a 'godsend' and how they hated washing up by hand. Unlike ourselves, Sam and Sal were very extraverted and relished having lots of friends over for food on a regular basis. We had observed that people in Portugal seemed to place great value on (as one of our Portuguese friends put it) 'conviviality': spending time with family and friends over home-cooked meals. The joy of hosting such a gathering is probably lessened somewhat if it is followed by three hours of washing up. Hence the worship of the dishwasher.

We returned from Ikea exhausted at the effort of shopping and trying to converse in Portuguese with Jorge and his wife, but triumphant at having finalized most of the big purchases. Two weeks later, the kitchen was finished and Jorge and his team had even put together most of the furniture for us. Jorge's wife, we were told, had insisted on cleaning the house from top to bottom before we moved in. She probably thought that we needed to save our strength for all that future dishwashing.

Sofia helped us to move our modest collection of personal belongings and small household items we had bought into the house. We gave her a tour of the garden before she left.

'Oh!' she said, standing on the terrace. 'I didn't realize this area was so close to the river. You have a fantastic view. How did you find this house?'

We explained that we had searched for houses online and had had no idea about the house's general siting and plot until we had come to Portugal to view it.

'You've managed to find yourself a *quintinha*,' she said.

She explained that the word *quinta* described a farm or a large estate; a *quintinha* was a 'little farm', a modest smallholding. And indeed the house's complicated layout, with its quirky sets of staircases and many internal doors, suggested that the footprint of the place had developed slowly over time, as new rooms and corridors were added. We liked the way that the little dwelling wasn't square, but a rough narrow diamond shape that snaked to the south, its face to the sun.

Although our small garden was very much an urban plot, we had high hopes of turning it into a productive kitchen garden. There was already an orange tree with, according to Jorge, very tasty fruit (we had noticed orange peel littering the garden on some of our visits to the house). And there were three grapevines, two red and one white. But aside for one or two ornamental plants, the tidy garden beds were a blank canvas. We sat on the patio on sunny January afternoons, admired the river, and drew up lists of plants and seeds we needed for the garden.

We also started to get acquainted with our neighbours, of whom we knew nothing. The day after we moved in, there was a loud knocking at the gate. I opened it to find a stocky woman who looked to be in her sixties. Her thick wavy hair was pulled back from her face in a hairband and she wore a spotless pink apron. She thrust a bunch of flowers into my hands.

'Bom dia! O meu nome é Beatriz,' she announced.

I attempted a hesitant 'Bom dia,' and told her our names.

She launched into what sounded like a prepared speech. She spoke quite slowly and enunciated carefully, so we were able to understand some of what she said. She had come round, she told us, to welcome us to the neighbourhood. She proceeded to gently interrogate us as to whether we had children, why we had moved to Portugal, and whether we already had family living there. When she learnt that we did not, she told us that we were to visit her house the next day for a cup of tea. She pointed to a large house further down the lane and made us repeat the designated time of our visit. Then she kissed us on the cheeks and left.

'I think we've just been adopted,' Geoff said.

'How sweet!' I said. 'I didn't think any of the neighbours would have noticed that we had moved in yet.'

But they had. The next day, there was another knock at the gate. This time it was a man and woman who introduced themselves as Susana and Roberto. Susana did all the talking, in fluent English. They lived just down the lane, she told us, with their son, Rui, who also spoke English. Roberto couldn't speak a work she revealed, laughing gaily, and translating rapidly for a rather embarrassed Roberto. She handed us a bag heavy with fruit: oranges, lemons, and tangerines from their garden, she explained. Before they left, Susana produced a slip of paper.

'This is our telephone number. If you need anything, anything at all, then please, you must call us.'

We felt somewhat overwhelmed at the kindness of our neighbours. On our previous visits to Portugal, we had been struck by the friendliness of the Portuguese people we had met. But visiting a country as a tourist and moving there permanently are two very different things. We had moved to a very old area of Gaia, one that was semi-rural and far from the tourist trail. We had had no idea how the sudden appearance of two *estrangeiros* would be received by the locals. But we needn't have worried. It seemed that this little community had decided to accept us.

Over the next few weeks, we had minor encounters with other of our neighbours. We had at least managed to master the phrases for greeting people, and were able to stutter out a *Bom dia*, *Boa tarde*, or *Boa noite* when we passed people on the lane.

One day, Geoff was outside on the lane brushing the area just outside our gate. An elderly man stopped and greeted him, then launched into an enthusiastic exchange about the house. He congratulated Geoff and shook his hand vigorously, pointing at the house and gate and giving a thumbs up. We gathered from this that our neighbours approved of the renovations to the house. They were probably relieved that the English (*os Ingleses*) hadn't made any unsympathetic or non-traditional changes such as building an ugly modern glass extension or installing a tumble dryer.

The day after Beatriz' visit, we called on her at the time she had specified. We were a little disconcerted to be met by a small welcome party. Beatriz introduced us to her husband, António, and two other neighbours, Maria and Lena, who looked at their new English neighbours with friendly curiosity.

Maria was a large, carefully turned out lady with an accent we found impenetrable and a throaty laugh. She had an air of relaxed ease about her. In contrast, everything about Lena was brisk and no nonsense, from her cropped hair to her tightly buttoned overall. Despite a bad limp, she moved with speed, as if she had no time for luxuries like pain. We liked them both immediately. After gently quizzing us about ourselves, Lena and Maria left, but not before pointing out their own houses, which were nearby.

Charming and urbane, with carefully dyed hair and a winning smile, António seemed delighted to welcome us as 'new friends'. He tagged along behind as Beatriz, resplendent in a floral dress and large gold earrings, ushered us up a flight of steps and into a large, high-ceilinged room. The area near the door contained two large sofas; towards the back of the room was a kitchen. In the middle was a huge dining table. This was set with a pretty porcelain tea service and vases of flowers. Various types of cakes and snacks were laid out ready.

Expecting a quick mug of tea, we had dressed down and come empty-handed. Abashed, we stammered out a few words of thanks. Beatriz waved them away and ushered us towards the table. However, António had other ideas. Smiling mischievously, he steered us gently towards a large cupboard in a corner of the room. He flung the carved wooden doors back to reveal a drinks cabinet filled with a wide range of different spirits and liquors.

'Wheesky?' he said. 'Aguadente, vodka, pastis?'

We declined. Neither of us felt like malt whisky at 2 o'clock in the afternoon on empty stomachs. António looked disappointed. He glumly surveyed the rows of bottles, most of which were full. They liked to keep a well-stocked drinks cabinet for visitors, he explained. But Beatriz only occasionally took a small glass of *ginja* (cherry brandy) for medicinal purposes and António only drank red wine from the Alentejo. And, alas, they had few visitors nowadays. He sighed heavily. Feeling guilty, we both accepted a glass of port and António cheered up immediately.

After a resplendent tea, Beatriz produced four fat photo albums and proceeded to give us a potted history of her family. We gazed at black and white photographs of Beatriz and António's wedding and of their four children. One of their sons lived in northern France and they had a daughter in London. A little regretfully, they showed us pictures of the whole family in the garden and gathered round the large table we were currently seated at. It was clear that they missed the busyness and conviviality of times long past. Nowadays, we gathered, Beatriz spent her time tending to her orchids and António walked to the cafe every afternoon to meet up with his friends and play cards.

Before we left, Beatriz insisted on giving us a complete tour of their house, which was more modern than our own. The design of our house suggested that it was built in the mid to late nineteenth century. The deeds to the house provided no real clues. The first large census in Portugal was in 1937, so the deeds for many houses built before 1937 bear this date, regardless of whether they were built in the sixteenth century or the early twentieth century. Beatriz' house seemed to date from the 1950s but as she led us round (after António had topped up our glasses), we were struck by their house's very traditional design.

All the living space was on one floor, which was reached by a long flight of steps. Off the large kitchen and living space was a narrow, dark corridor which gave onto four small bedrooms, also quite dark. Another large family room at the back of the house opened onto the garden.

Most of the ground floor was taken up by a large cellar and after refilling our glasses, António led us down there. We gathered that this was his domain. A large wine press, now dusty with disuse, dominated the room. Rows of demijohns stood empty on the shelves that lined the walls. The garden still contained two mature grapevines but it seemed that these were no longer used to produce wine. António shook his head sadly. He was too old for all that, he declared. It was all in the past now.

Cheering up, he led us to a large wooden wine rack filled with numerous bottles of red wine. Apparently, his winemaking energies were now channelled into collecting choice vintages of the full-bodied red wine from the mid and south of Portugal. Before we went back upstairs, he generously insisted on selecting a bottle for us to take home.

Much later that afternoon we strolled home, both of us quiet and slightly overwhelmed at the generosity of our new neighbours. Beatriz and António had opened their hearts and their home (and their photo albums) to us. And we got the impression that our other neighbours were quite pleased to have two exotic newcomers in their midst. We felt sure that the long relationship between Portugal and Britain had helped in this respect. The two countries have one of the oldest alliances between any two countries in the world. Beatriz had proudly shown us her modest collection of British memorabilia, which consisted of a small plastic model of Big Ben, a chipped mug commemorating the marriage of Prince Charles to Lady Diana Spencer, and, curiously, a tea towel depicting the words of Auld Lang Syne.

With the house renovations finished and the connections we were beginning to forge with our new community, we felt we were finally settling in to our new life. Now all we had to do was work out how to earn some money.

8

One of the reasons we chose to move to Portugal was the lower cost of living the country offered. We had read that council tax, water bills, and electricity costs were much lower than in the UK. Nevertheless, we still needed some kind of income. We had ruled out trying to find employment in Portugal. The country has a high rate of unemployment and, as English academics who were not fluent in Portuguese, we were unlikely to secure jobs in a Portuguese university. Anyway, we had had more than our fill of academia; we wanted a complete change.

We decided we would try to make a living writing. After years of writing papers for scientific journals we were eager to do something different. Although writing and publishing is a large part of an academic's job, scholarly research and writing is hugely shaped by university publication targets and what type of research is funded. Now free of these constraints, we excitedly planned a rather ambitious set of writing projects, from novels to non-fiction books that further explored our more academic interests.

However, writing books takes time and we were acutely aware that, providing we spent the absolute minimum, we had only about two years worth of savings left. Happily, along with the cut in our income, we now had drastically reduced outgoings. We had realized while still in Wales that living off the system wasn't necessarily a cheap option. The remoteness of our cottage in the hills meant that we had to run a four-wheel drive vehicle. The calor gas bottles we used for cooking and running the gas lamps weren't cheap, and we spent about fifteen hundred pounds each year on logs for the wood burner, which had to be lit almost every day to keep the cottage warm and dry.

We hoped that the sunnier climate in Portugal meant that we would spend less on heating and that our small solar system would produce a decent amount of power. And better weather would surely improve our chances of growing our own fruit and vegetables, thus cutting down on food bills.

Another expense that we no longer had was running a car. Towards the top of our wish list when house-hunting in Portugal had been to find a place with good transport links. We knew that, for the first few years at least, we wouldn't be able to afford to buy even a second-hand car, so the simplest and cheapest option was to try and do without one altogether. The bus stop was only a short walk from the house, as were a range of local shops. It was ironic that now we were living in the city and (mostly) on the system, our cost of living was much lower than it had been living off-grid in North Wales.

Most importantly, we didn't have to worry about house rent or repayments. Portugal was one of the few places in Europe where the house prices were cheap enough to allow us to be mortgage-free. In those early weeks, with the stress of the move and the renovation fading, we often sat on our freshly tiled patio looking at the river and congratulating ourselves on finding such a bargain.

However, not all the locals agreed with us. We had

popped round to Beatriz' one day to find that her youngest son, Tiago, was visiting. He welcomed us warmly and apologized for his poor grasp of English. In fact, he spoke English fluently and he chatted away enthusiastically, translating for Beatriz every couple of minutes. During the course of the conversation he confided that it was a shame we had paid so much for the house, and alluded to the ruthless nature of estate agents nowadays. We were astonished. We told him that we thought the house had been a snip at the equivalent of fifty-two thousand pounds, and explained that a similar sized house with an attractive river view in Liverpool would have been six times the price. He blew his cheeks out in incredulity, but we suspected he still thought we were mad.

We had a similar response from the old gentleman who lived across the lane. The steep slope of the land meant that this neighbour's plot was roughly at the level of our low roofline. He lived in a large ramshackle house that was in even worse repair than our own had been. It stood in a spacious garden that contained several beautiful old trees, including an enormous oak. Blue wisteria covered one crumbling wall of the house, and the tiles edging the roof were held in place by thick green lichen.

Tall and gaunt, with a rather distinguished-looking high forehead and a slightly hooked nose, the old man seemed friendly enough. We always waved as we passed if he was in his garden, which he was most of the time. We had even exchanged a few words over the garden wall, although his voice was heavily accented and he was difficult to follow. As we didn't know his name, we referred to him, between ourselves, as Alta Man, his land being *mais alta*, higher than, our own.

One day, we were walking back from the bus stop when we happened upon Alta Man, who was pruning the grapevine that hung over the wall near his front gate. He hailed us and we stopped for a chat. We told him that we had been shopping in Porto. He shook his head and gestured towards his garden. He never went into Porto nowadays he said; he was far too busy. He told us that his wife had died a few years ago and now it was just him and his daughter, Maria. His face darkened. She didn't like gardening, he said. And indeed, we had never seen his daughter, either in the garden or on the lane, and had assumed that Alta Man lived alone.

Alta Man asked us both our ages then pointed to himself. 'Tenho noventa e um anos,' he said proudly.

We were impressed. Ninety-one! We had assumed he was in his late sixties. Working in his garden, his movements were those of a much younger man, and when he walked down the lane his back was ramrod straight.

We turned to take our leave and Alta Man gestured towards our house. It was a nice little house, he said, but, alas, we had paid far too much for it. The house was *muito cara*, Alta Man declared, very expensive.

We insisted that we thought our house was very cheap. We pointed out to Alta Man that *em Ingleterre*, the houses were much more expensive.

Alta Man shook his head sadly and placed a hand comfortingly on each of our shoulders. His sympathetic glance seemed to say, 'You poor gullible English fools!' We left clutching a large bag of lemons from Alta Man's garden, bemused at our apparent reputation for buying expensive real estate.

The elevated position of his garden allowed Alta Man a vantage point from which to survey most of the happenings on our lane. As he was in his garden almost every day, he could monitor most of the goings on in the neighbourhood. If we were doing any maintenance work to the front of the house, Alta Man would pop up out of the greenery, secateurs or hoe in hand, like some benign spirit of the place. At the other end of the lane, Beatriz kept a beady eye on the neighbourhood from her balcony. Between them, Beatriz and Alta Man had the kind of surveillance coverage that MI5 could only dream of.

Alta Man's well-intentioned but rather zealous policing of the local tradespeople and services meant that we dreaded the occasions when we needed to hire someone to do some work on the place. Alta Man would stare down from his garden and if he could, engage any visiting worker in conversation. Then he would interrogate them about how much they were charging to do the work in question. Jorge had given us the number of Nuno, one of his friends who cleaned out and maintained septic tanks, and we arranged for the man to come and empty our own *fossa*. While we were opening the back gate in preparation, Alta Man hailed Nuno and started his usual barrage of questions. By the time we reappeared at the front gate, poor Nuno was unreeling his heavy pipe as fast as he could and trying to ignore Alta Man, who from the safety of the garden was scolding 'Muito caro, muito caro!' and wagging a long thin finger at Nuno.

Alta Man himself flatly refused to pay anyone to work on his own house, which of course was why it was falling down around his ears. We eventually discovered that Alta Man's name was Fernando. Although we called him Senhor Fernando to his face, between ourselves we still referred to him as Alta Man. In those early weeks, when we had yet to get to know all of our neighbours properly, we assigned them names that helped us to distinguish them and remember who was who.

Unfortunately, those early (rather flippant) names have stuck and we still use them today. This is partly because there is so much overlap in personal names between our neighbours. When we lived in North Wales, we followed the local practice of referring to our neighbours by the names of their houses, because the surnames of almost all the families in the village were Jones, Evans, or Williams. Our Portuguese neighbours had a similarly restricted range of first names.

Almost all the women in our neighbourhood seemed to be called Maria or Ana, and almost all the men were João or António.

The locals, we learnt, had their own methods for avoiding confusion over names. A subtle nod of the head or a tilt of the chin towards the person's house was used to indicate who you were referring to. Alternately, a descriptor could be added to the name. So our neighbour Maria, who we had met at Beatriz' house, was often referred to as Dona Maria. She was one of the oldest Marias in the neighbourhood, and *Dona* is a polite respectful title often given to older ladies. In contrast, Alta Man's daughter, who was one of the youngest Marias in the area, was referred to as Mariazinha. The diminutive *inho* or *inha* is often used to indicate a smaller version of something, as in *cafezinho* or *quintinha*.

Next to the nearby *lavadouro* was a tiny half-ruin of a house, picturesque in its decay. Several of the mellow terracotta roof tiles were cracked and the render was crumbling from the walls. On the upper storey there was one window and a door that led out onto a small patio. The lower storey seemed to be just a cellar. In this tumbledown dwelling lived an elderly man who looked even older than Alta Man. As the tumbledown house was *mais baixa*, lower down, than our own house, we called its occupant Baixa Man.

Each day, Baixa Man would emerge from his gloomy

home to catch some sun on the patio. He would stand and gaze for a while at the river and at his unruly garden, which he rarely ventured into. If we were in our garden, we would exchange smiles and waves. Once or twice we had encountered Baixa Man on the lane, out for a stroll. Our attempts at conversation were unsuccessful; although an enthusiastic conversationalist, Baixa Man was impossible to understand as he had hardly any teeth. Our contribution to these rather one-sided conversations was limited to nodding and smiling, and the occasional *Sim* or *Não* in what we hoped were the right places.

Despite his harmless appearance, Baixa Man had a disturbing habit. Every so often, he would collect up all the bits of rubbish that the wind had blown down into the *lavadouro*, pile it into a corner, and set fire to it. The smoke would drift up into our garden and if we had hung washing out to dry, would necessitate a panicked dash to collect it in before the smoke reached it. Even if there was no washing to worry about, the toxic nature of Baixa Man's fires meant that it was impossible to work in the garden or have any windows open while they were burning. The small garbage mountains Baixa Man constructed were composed of plastic bags, milk cartons, old shoes ... basically anything that shouldn't be burnt was fair game for his bonfires.

The first time it had happened, we had thought there was a house fire somewhere. We peered down from the terrace through the plumes of heavy acrid smoke to see Baixa Man hunched over his little blaze, poking the contents with a long stick. He gazed up at us, eyes bright, and gave a friendly little wave.

'He's sweet,' I said to Geoff. 'He doesn't mean any harm; he's just trying to keep the place tidy.'

'He's a little firebug,' responded Geoff. 'He knows he shouldn't be lighting fires this time of year.'

The ever-present threat of wild fires in Portugal means that there are strict rules on burning greenery at certain times of the year to reduce the risk of uncontrolled blazes. Despite this, we had noticed that the bonfire was the preferred solution for many of our neighbours to dispose of all the green garden waste their sizeable plots generated (the other solution being to stuff the three communal rubbish bins with twigs, leaves, and grass). Composting, it seemed, was considered esoteric nonsense.

One day, we showed Beatriz our newly installed compost bin. Beatriz and António had a large garden so we assumed they probably had a row of compost bins. But no. Beatriz regarded our pile of slowly rotting green waste with puzzlement and not a little distaste.

'But why?' she asked. She pointed over in the direction of the rubbish bins. 'We use those,' she pointed out gently.

And indeed we had seen Beatriz laboriously dragging long thin branches of vine and other plants down the lane to the bins.

We had once seen a feature on the modern novelty of garden composting on a local television news programme. A gardening 'expert' had been invited in to explain the concept, and several compost bins of different sizes and styles had been set up in a garden. The expert was pointing out their merits to a small group of gardeners, all men, who were gazing at the compost bins with suspicion. Before the feature ended the expert handed the men a leaflet each about composting methods. They examined their leaflets appreciatively.

'They're wondering how well those leaflets will burn,' Geoff said. 'They'll go straight on the bonfire when they get home.'

He was probably right.

There was only one thing that curtailed Baixa Man's

pyromaniac tendencies, and that was the presence of the ladies of the *lavadouro*. Cláudia had told us that in Portugal, most parishes have several wash-houses, or *lavadouros*. These stone or concrete structures are often very old, but new ones are sometimes built to service apartment blocks or new housing developments. In the past, these communal areas were central to the lives of working class women, and were spaces in which both work and social interactions were carried out. In her fascinating study of abandoned *lavadouros* in Porto, the architect and researcher Chloé Darmon argues that these public wash-houses are 'an integral part of the culture and memory' of cities like Porto.

Our local *lavadouro* consisted of two large tanks; a 'dirty' tank to wash clothes in and a 'clean' tank for rinsing. A simple roof covered the tanks so that they could be used in all weathers. These structures are usually built around a natural spring so that the water is constantly refreshed. Like our own smaller tank in the garden, the sides of the large tanks provide a slightly sloping surface on which one can rub the clothes vigorously while the water drains away.

From our garden we often heard the shouts and singing of the local women (and it was always women) who used the *lavadouro*. We had seen them brushing up the detritus of Baixa Man's bonfires, and scolding him in no uncertain terms about his little hobby.

We always felt too shy to go down to the *lavadouro* on a busy washing day. But one cold winter day, we could hear no activity so we ventured down the little flight of cobbled steps to look around. The clear water in the two tanks was calm but a gentle ripple under the surface indicated the presence of the inflow of water from the spring. Sunlight dappled the surface of the water and the ripples reflected back onto the *lavadouro* roof.

‘It must be miserable washing down here at this time of year,’ I said. ‘The water must be freezing.’ I dipped a finger into one of the tanks. ‘It’s warm!’

‘Is it?’ Geoff did the same, then he grinned. ‘Of course, it would be, wouldn’t it? It’s an underground spring. The water will stay at pretty much the same temperature all year round.’

He was right. Just like the spring near our cottage in Wales, this ancient water source came from deep underground, ensuring that the *lavadouro* water was always at a comfortable temperature.

Although the *lavadouro* was now empty, someone had obviously been busy that morning. A set of freshly washed towels had been carefully laid out to dry on the flat top of a stone wall that bordered the *lavadouro* area. A red and white striped wash bag sat ready in a corner by the tank, waiting for the owner of the towels to return.

We wandered over to inspect the spring. A large stone edifice bearing the date 1904 had been constructed to one side of the *lavadouro*. The stone was worn and some of the pointing was loose but the carvings on the stone were attractive. A rusting metal pipe emerged from this rather grand façade and from it flowed the spring, falling with some force into a stone basin beneath. We dabbled our fingers in the clear water, welcoming its warmth on this cold day.

A loud voice from behind made us jump. We turned to see a tall elderly woman with unruly curly hair carrying a large rug. She dropped her rug on the stone sill of the water tanks and came over to us. We wished her a polite *Boa tarde*. In reply she launched into an enthusiastic torrent of words, grabbed my shoulders and planted a kiss on each cheek, then did the same to Geoff. Bemused, we could only smile and stand there nodding like idiots, for she was even harder to understand than Baixa Man.

We eventually worked out that she was asking us the usual questions: what were our names, how old were we, did we have children? She stabbed a finger at her own chest and told us that she was eighty-two and that her name was Matilde. She pointed out her own house, and declared that she had lived in the neighbourhood for sixty years. The air was pure here, she said; it was a good place to live and she knew we would like it.

We asked if the water was clean to drink. Yes, yes, she nodded. To emphasize her point, she took us both by the hand and led us to the spring outlet. She cupped a hand under the flow and brought it her lips. See! It was very good, she said. She herself had been drinking it all her life, and look how strong she was! She curled her biceps and grinned, showing several missing teeth. We smiled, polite but sceptical. But then Matilde produced four 6-litre plastic bottles, of the kind you buy mineral water in, and proceeded to fill them from the spring. When Geoff moved in to help lift the filled bottles she waved him away. She did this every day, she said, it was easy! She lifted the bottles, two in each hand, as if they were empty. I goggled. I couldn't have done that when I was twenty!

I stared at the spring then muttered to Geoff, 'What is this, the fountain of youth or something?'

We left Matilde vigorously scrubbing her rug and slowly walked back up the steps to the road, puffing slightly. We were both thinking the same thing. The sooner we started drinking that spring water, the better.

9

With the house now renovated (as much as we could afford, anyway), we were at last ready to begin turning our ideas into actual books and hopefully making some kind of living. Satisfying as it was to sit in our sunny little house, free of the distractions of university life, the prospect of making any money from writing seemed a long way off.

However, what we lacked in income we made up for in time. This gave us the opportunity to try and learn more about our adopted city. And we discovered that there was plenty to explore close at hand. We could see why many of our neighbours hardly ever went into central Gaia, let alone Porto. We could also see why they looked so fit. Much of Porto and Gaia is hilly and our neighbourhood was no exception. You could find most of the shops and services you might need within walking distance, but you had to work for it. Many of the lanes were steep and cobbled, which made walking hard work. The first few longer walking trips we took left us with well-toned calf muscles and sore ankles.

But it was a pleasure, on a clear sunny morning, to wander up the steep lane near our house, pausing at the top to gaze at the panorama of the River Douro stretched out before us.

Turning, we would carry on down the narrow lane, past the public fountain and the gaggle of cats sunning themselves on the stone cobbles. Rounding a bend, the lane wound on upwards. Here, at this spot near a crumbling stone wall, there was always a pile of fallen horse chestnuts in the autumn. A little further on, the walk was shaded by the overhanging branches of a large orange tree, and the scent of orange blossom filled the air.

As the lane widened, it levelled out and you could slow your pace and catch your breath. You could even sit and have a coffee or a cold beer, as the first of the five small cafes within walking distance was situated on the corner opposite the small field where a few of the neighbours grazed their goats. Keep going (if your calf muscles allow it) just a little further and you will find yourself on the main shopping strip, the 'Big Smoke', which affords a *mini-mercado*, a hardware shop, a florists, a butchers shop, and a hairdressers.

Do not be deceived into thinking that these shops offer a limited range of goods. The *mini-mercado* might look like a small corner shop, the kind that sells a few overpriced groceries and little else. But in Portugal, these small unassuming establishments are emporiums of all manner of different products. Our own *mini-mercado* was no exception. Despite being tiny, it sold a large range of local fruit and vegetables, fresh eggs, cheese and ham (sold by the slice), tinned and frozen goods, toiletries, a selection of beers and wines, and freshly baked cakes and bread.

It was run by an energetic lady called Mrs Costa, who to our surprise, greeted us by name the first time we ventured in there. All became clear when we found out that she was a friend of Beatriz. News travelled fast in our neighbourhood, but if Beatriz was involved, it was conveyed at the speed of light.

Mrs Costa's *mini-mercado* wasn't just the best source of fresh produce, it was an important local hub of community activity. People sat under the mimosa tree in the tiny square opposite her shop and gathered in the shop on Fridays, when she had her main food delivery, to exchange gossip. For us, it required a certain amount of bravery to tackle Mrs Costa's on a busy afternoon. The tiny shop would be crammed with customers and if the bread man or the egg man turned up with their deliveries, it was chaos. You had to flatten yourself against the veg racks and duck if you saw a wooden tray full of fragrant bread rolls coming your way. Alternately you could escape into Mrs Costa's back room, which smelt of candle wax and laundry soap.

It didn't help that many of Mrs Costa's more elderly female customers liked to linger in the shop chatting after they had done their shopping. They would install themselves on the hard-backed chair near the counter or even on the step leading into the back room. With their stuffed shopping bags arrayed around their ankles, they could keep up a running commentary to Mrs Costa and any of her customers who wanted to join in. As far as we could make out, their discussions usually consisted of complaints about their husbands and their daughters-in-law, diatribes against the local council, and lamentations about the rising price of bus fares.

We were unfamiliar with some of these ladies, as they didn't live on our lane. They would smile at us and occasionally pat us on the arm, friendly but a little wary of the *estrangeiros*. I think many of them assumed we could speak no Portuguese at all, but when we were brave enough to make a comment or two in Portuguese they would laugh delightedly and then launch into the kind of fast, impassioned chatter that we had no hope at all of understanding. It was then our turn to smile warily and try to edge out of the shop as politely as possible.

Sometimes, a brave fellow customer might try out on us whatever non-Portuguese expression they had happened to pick up. So we might tentatively enter Mrs Costa's on a busy morning to be startled by a loud '*Bonjour*!' or '*Guten Morgen*!'. We usually responded in kind, and then followed it with 'Good morning', as it seemed churlish to deflate their enthusiasm by pointing out that they had picked the wrong language.

One day, we decided to call in at Senhor Pereira's hardware shop, which was just down the lane from the *mini-mercado*. I had been perusing the glass cabinet in which Mrs Costa displayed toiletries, looking for lip balm. Alas, she said, she was out of stock, but I would certainly be able to find some at Senhor Pereira's.

When we got outside, I said to Geoff, 'My Portuguese pronunciation must be getting worse!'

'What do you mean?'

'I thought I pronounced *balsamo labial* quite well. But she must have misheard me. I seriously doubt that the hardware shop stocks lip balm.'

'Let's call in and see,' Geoff suggested. 'Gives us a chance to have a look around.'

Entering Senhor Pereira's shop, we realized that the modest frontage, which was covered with pretty yellow tiles, disguised what was actually a huge space. Although the shop was narrow, it seemed to go back a long way. Behind the L-shaped counter, loaded shelves receded into the gloom. A forest of household items dangled from ceiling hooks: wicker log baskets, oil lamps, laundry bags, and other essentials. Against the walls stood galvanized metal mop buckets, large garden planters, and what looked like the national collection of brooms.

A wide staircase led up to a second floor. On this warm

afternoon, the shop appeared empty. But as we were looking round for a bell to ring, Senhor Pereira suddenly appeared behind the counter. Whether he had been sitting there all the time or had glided silently from the dark reaches of the back of the shop we had no idea.

Senhor Pereira was a short stocky man with neat silver hair and a small moustache. Kind blue eyes glinted from behind his thick glasses. We had seen his wife, Senhora Pereira, once or twice when passing the shop and she had greeted us cheerily. We knew that the Pereiras lived above the shop because on fine days a clothes airer hung with washing dangled underneath one of the upstairs windows.

At the back of the shop was a spacious yard enclosed by a high wall and accessed through double metal gates. In the daytime, the gates were open and if you glanced in as you passed you would see an interesting collection of large oil and water tanks (for sale), myriad terracotta pots filled with begonias, more washing hanging to dry, and a large goose. Whether the goose was a pet or a guard animal, we didn't know, but it marched up and down the yard quacking gustily.

None of the hardware shops we had frequented in the UK had a resident goose. Neither did they stock the dizzying range of goods that the Pereiras did. My hesitant inquiry about *balsamo labial* was met with a nod and a smile by Senhor Pereira and he directed me to a glass-topped counter in which were displayed a wide range of lip balms, hand and face creams, manicure sets, hair nets, and nail polish. But Senhor Pereira had not forgotten his male customers. Next to this collection were displayed a selection of shaving brushes, shaving soap, hair oil, and beautifully polished tobacco pipes.

As Senhor Pereira was carefully wrapping the lip balm in a bit of paper, we gazed at some of the goods displayed behind the counter. A tall rack of pans reflected in their shiny surfaces the collection of door knobs artfully arranged on a small table next to them. Behind the table stood several charcoal barbecues and next to them there was a large wooden crate filled with furry slippers. The general impression was that of a Turkish bazaar. I imagined that if I were to wander through the maze of shadowy shelves to the back of the shop, I would probably be able to find a dolly tub and a mangle in good working order.

In North Wales, we had struggled to find gas mantles and chamber pots to use in our primitive off-grid cottage. I suspected that these old-fashioned items would be easy to find at Senhor Pereira's.

We bought two lip balms, a garden brush, some wooden clothes pegs, and a new hammer. As we were leaving, Geoff spotted some very large robust plant pots, which were priced very cheaply. But we were laden down with our purchases from Mrs Costa's. When we mentioned to Senhor Pereira that we would return the next day to buy some pots, he told us not to worry. His son lived round the corner from us, he said, and would happily deliver them to our door. Everyone in the area, it seemed, knew who we were and where we lived!

Our little neighbourhood of maze-like streets was the oldest part of the parish. We had driven with Pedro through what turned out to be the modern centre of the parish and we realized that this was just a short bus ride, or a moderate walk, away. This area contained an impressively large old church and graveyard. There were two old *quintas* and some scattered cottages. Around these had grown a more modern settlement that included a school, a bank, a post office, and a supermarket. But there were still plenty of smaller characterful shops and cafes.

One autumn day, we decided to take the bus up to the

parish centre. Alighting, we looked round for a suitable cafe. Nearby was an attractive cobbled square that boasted a large and beautiful jacaranda tree. A few tables and chairs were set out under the tree. These seemed to belong to a large bakery and patisserie. We remembered that Beatriz had waxed lyrical about this bakery and had once brought us a box of *pasteis de nata* after one of her frequent trips there.

An enticing smell of baked bread and freshly brewed coffee greeted us as we entered. Inside, wooden tables and chairs were set out in front of a very long glass counter containing a huge range of cakes, pastries, and savoury *lanches*. Behind the counter, an array of baskets displayed baguettes, bread rolls, *pão da avó* (literally, 'grandmother's bread'), heavy dark corn bread, and other local varieties. At either end of the long counter stood tall glass cabinets, their shelves crammed with elaborate tarts and rich gateaux. After ordering cake and coffee we went to sit outside under the jacaranda tree.

Watching a blue blossom float gently to the ground, I said to Geoff, 'I don't know about you, but I'm happy to spend the whole afternoon here.'

Geoff gazed at the enormous slice of chocolate gateaux that had just been placed on our table. 'I agree. After I've eaten this, I may not be able to move for some time.'

I picked a strawberry off the top of my own slice of cake. 'This is the life.'

And indeed it was. We sat there listening to the low murmur of the old men at the next table playing cards, and were thoroughly content. Our little parish was perfectly ordinary; it possessed no fancy restaurants or hotels and wasn't on the tourist trail. But, perhaps because of that, it was full of life, full of interest. Maybe it was the cafes on every street corner, the chatter of the women down at the *lavadouros*, or the tiny shops that had somehow managed to survive the influx of the supermarkets. But we sensed the energy of a community that was still mostly in touch with its traditions.

When it arrived, the bill for our spectacular coffee and cake was ridiculously low. We spent a pleasant afternoon wandering round the little parish centre. Before we left, we stocked up on figs and olives from the fruit and veg shop then returned to the bakery to buy some *pasteis de nata* for Beatriz. As it was sunny with a light warm breeze, we decided to walk back home rather than catch the bus. We walked back past the old *quinta*, admiring the birdsong and the bougainvillea spilling over the high wall surrounding its lush garden.

'We need to get some bougainvillea for the garden,' I said.

'Mmm. And a fig tree. And an olive tree,' Geoff said.

Our mental list of plants and trees we wanted for the garden was now enormous. Beatriz had given us some rose cuttings but we wanted food as well as flowers. The trouble was, we were having difficulty finding garden supplies. In the UK, we regularly visited garden centres and specialist nurseries, and bought both ordinary and heritage seeds online. In Portugal, our searches in Gaia and Porto city centres, and online, had proved fruitless. It seemed that garden centres were not popular in Portugal.

A thought occurred to me. 'We should ask Beatriz where she gets her plants from,' I said.

Beatriz had become our local fount of all knowledge. She freely offered us advice (whether we had asked for it or not) on a huge range of topics, from the best place to buy apples to the best way to cook beans.

When we got home from our walk, I took the little box of *natas* round to Beatriz'. As she put the kettle on the hob, she announced that she was taking us on a trip the following day. Every Thursday, there was a large local market in the neighbouring parish. She had booked a taxi already and we were to be at her gate at 9 am sharp.

'I don't want spend all day shopping,' Geoff grumbled when I told him.

'It's a *fait accompli,*' I said. 'She's already booked Manuel.'

'Who?'

'The taxi driver. A friend of hers, apparently.'

'She really does know everyone round here doesn't she? Is António going?'

'I suppose so. I expect he has no choice in the matter.'

'I guess it will be interesting to see one of the local markets,' Geoff said.

But when we arrived at Beatriz' the next morning she informed us that António wasn't coming. Apparently, he was meeting some friends at the cafe. He hated shopping, she said. Geoff looked at me meaningfully.

Hastily changing the subject, I said to Beatriz, in Portuguese, 'Are you taking both of those?'

She had wheeled two shopping trolleys to the gate. The larger of the two was of red and blue tartan. The smaller trolley, which apparently was for us to use, was white with a rather garish design of hot pink flowers.

Geoff grinned at me. 'I'll let you pull that,' he smirked.

'I don't know why we need those,' I muttered to Geoff, as Beatriz closely supervised Manuel as he loaded the two trolleys into the boot of the car.

But Beatriz' plan soon became clear. In the taxi, she told us that we were going to spend most of the day at the little market, with a break for lunch in a cafe that she liked in the village square. Our hearts sank. Except for the Conwy honey fair, which we tried to attend every year, the markets we were used to in the UK were uninspiring affairs, consisting mainly of a couple of basic fruit and veg stalls and an acre of stalls selling cheap clothing and shoes. The prospect of spending a whole day trailing Beatriz round one of these markets was less than thrilling.

However, we soon realized that this market was different. Leading off the village square was a long broad lane which had been closed to traffic on this market day. Along the edges of the lane were set up stalls piled high with a huge range of goods: hand-woven baskets, garden tools, colourful crockery, dried flowers. It was true that amongst this eclectic bazaar were one or two stalls hawking cut-price clothes and bags, but they were in the minority. We strolled down the gently sloping lane, which eventually widened out into a large cobbled plaza shaded by mature trees. This, it seemed, was the heart of the market. Here, set out on two large terraces were many more stalls, broadly organized according to their wares.

It was pleasant to stroll and browse in the dappled light under the trees. We walked past stalls laden with jars of honey, admiring the way the sunlight intensified the golds, ambers, and caramels of their contents. Enticing aromas drew us through the baked goods section, where we were tempted by fat loaves of *pão de avó* and freshly baked biscuits. We spent too long deliberating over the different vats of juicy olives and the beautifully arranged regional cheeses.

In the fruit and vegetable section, we bought bags of cherries to snack on and watched the elderly ladies sitting with their hand mincers preparing bags of shredded cabbage, which is an important ingredient in the ubiquitous *caldo verde* soup. A fragrant haze of roasting chestnuts hung in the air and as we walked, stallholders pressed delicacies into our hands: bits of São Jorge cheese, almond biscuits, soft slices of pear.

A cacophony of squeaks and quacks signified that we were approaching the pet and livestock section. The stalls in this part of the market were bigger, with frameworks that supported broad canopies to shade the animals from the sun. Some were festooned with cages of brightly coloured canaries and finches. Songbirds are popular in Portugal and many of our neighbours kept them. When the weather was fine the cages were brought outside and hung in the garden or on a balcony for the birds to enjoy the sunshine. Alta Man had several such birds and their lovely song often drifted down to our own garden.

After listening to the songbirds we went and cooed over the little enclosures that housed the chicks, little round bundles of feathers and feet, and the soft-eyed rabbits. It is not unusual in Portugal to keep a few chickens or rabbits for food, even in the city. The family we had bought our house from had obviously kept rabbits, as the lower garden contained a set of large stone cages fronted with chicken wire. For us, they provided excellent storage for plant pots and spare roof tiles.

I found myself falling in love with the delicate looking quail chicks. 'We need some of those,' I told Geoff.

'No we don't' he said. 'We need plants first.'

Beatriz seemed surprised when we asked her if the market sold plants. 'Claro,' she said and gestured for us to follow her.

She led us through what seemed to be an outdoor eating area. Tables and chairs were set out by a little fountain. Several food carts and vans provided an eclectic choice of dishes for hungry market-goers. Fish lovers could dine on grilled *sardinhas* or *bacalhau*, *bifanas* of marinaded pork in a hefty sandwich, or spicy *piri piri* chicken. If you wanted a lighter snack, there were *lanches* galore, warm and stuffed with meat, vegetables, or cheese, or sweet *churros* and *farturas*. We lingered, our mouths watering, but Beatriz explained that we were going to get a late lunch later in her favourite cafe. When Beatriz had her mind set on something it was best to acquiesce, so we followed her past the food stalls and round a corner into a quiet little area shaded by three enormous chestnut trees.

We were expecting to find one or two plant stalls. Instead, there were about thirty market pitches, selling everything from trees and shrubs to small charcoal barbecues. There were seeds and bulbs for sale, and even trays of late-season brassica plants. The markets, it seemed, were where you bought your garden supplies in Portugal. While Beatriz browsed the houseplants, we shopped for trees and herbs, trying to work out what we could feasibly fit into the taxi. In the end, we limited ourselves to a small lime tree, a young apple tree, a few raspberry canes, and several pots of herbs. We made a mental note to revisit the market as soon as possible.

It turned out that Beatriz had been wise to bring the shopping trolleys. We slowly made our way up the hill to the square, pulling trolleys laden with food, plants, and other purchases, and carrier bags stuffed with plants and trees. Beatriz couldn't resist lingering to look at the jewellery. We left her comparing three identical-looking fine gold chains, pursing her lips at the prices, and wandered over to a large haberdashery stall that boasted an imaginative display of buttons of all shapes and colours. As a birthday gift, my mother had recently bought me a sewing machine. I looked longingly at the huge variety of fabrics on sale, all of which seemed like bargains, but alas, we were spent up for the day and eager for lunch.

In the cafe in the square, we ate fluffy omelettes followed by strawberry tarts and coffee. Before we left, we couldn't resist purchasing a selection of the handmade chocolates that the cafe produced. Beatriz also bought a box of cakes for António, which we guessed was a sweetener for when she showed him the gold chain she had bought.

As we sat in the square in the sunshine waiting for Manuel to pick us up, I asked Beatriz if he would mind us filling his car boot with plants. She told me that he was used to her market trips. Besides, she had bought him a large profiterole as a treat, so she was sure he would be '*muito contente*'!

10

One day, we had a telephone call from Henrique. A minor administrative issue had come up about our tax documents. Henrique proposed that we meet up at Finanças, the tax office, and then go for lunch in Porto. We suspected that Henrique's preference for carrying out all his business face to face (preferably over lunch) went a long way to explaining his chronic lateness. We arranged to meet him in a cafe on Avenida dos Aliados, and started to collect our documents together.

We had noticed that people in Portugal often carried round with them little plastic folders full of documentation when they went somewhere like the bank or the doctor's surgery. We had wondered about these folders and assumed that Portuguese people were just super-organized. But as we became more familiar with the extent of bureaucracy in Portugal the folders suddenly made sense. A relatively simple administrative task, such as renewing a driving licence or applying for a supermarket loyalty card, can often require a bewildering array of documentation, and it isn't always easy to predict in advance which documents will be needed.

We had learnt the hard way that relatively simple

procedures like registering at the local health centre can easily require three or four attempts, due to these esoteric administrative requirements. We therefore started to adopt the Portuguese strategy of stuffing a document folder with almost all the personal documents we possessed when visiting places such as the bank, the tax office, or the hospital.

We were gratified to find that previously stern officials would visibly relax when we produced, without being asked, fiscal numbers, bank statements, and other bumpf. We now played the system at its own game. When faced with a dour-looking official, we overwhelmed them with paperwork.

Almost an hour after the arranged time, Henrique turned up and our business at Finanças was concluded. We lingered over a late lunch. Henrique was eager to find out how we were settling into our new home. When we told him that we were about to receive our first visitors (our mothers), Henrique's eyes lit up. 'I would be happy to show you and your mothers some of the hidden places of Porto,' he said.

We hesitated. Tempting as the offer was, we had no wish to spend a week waiting around for a stressed Henrique to turn up. It was a kind gesture on his part, but we knew he didn't really have the time and had no wish to make his already frantic schedule worse.

'It's very generous of you,' said Geoff, 'but we couldn't. We know how busy you are.'

Henrique smiled graciously. I thought he looked distinctly relieved.

In fact, we had managed to find our own favourite corners of the city, often well off the beaten track, and had become experts in exploring on the cheap. Part of what had drawn us to Porto in the first place was the city's unique spirit. Even on our earlier holidays, we had sought out the back streets, the local, and the more obscure corners of the city, the better to soak up the atmosphere of the place. Now we had the time to extend our observations. And the imminent visit of the Mums was a perfect opportunity to show off some of Porto's lesser-known charms.

Of course, the Mums would want to see some of the more famous sights of Porto, such as Sé do Porto (the city's impressive cathedral), Rua de Santa Catarina, and the Ribeira district. But we planned to introduce our visitors to some of the more quirky corners of the city. In our wanderings, we had stumbled across many interesting spots, often by chance.

One warm day, for instance, we caught the bus from Avenida da República over the river to Porto to spend a lazy afternoon mooching around the city. From the bus we saw what looked like lots of activity at Alameda das Fontainhas, an area overlooking the river. Curious, we alighted at the next stop and walked down the hill to see what was going on.

To our delight, it was a little flea market. A gloriously chaotic jumble of stalls filled the flat boulevard. Some pitches were just tarpaulins or blankets laid on the ground. The mood was relaxed and cheerful, and indeed this was the perfect place for a market. People milled around, inspecting the displays of second-hand books, clothes, crockery, and various types of bric-a-brac. Some had purchased snacks or drinks from the street food vendors and were leaning on the wall to gaze at the river below. Although it was only mid-morning the outdoor tables of the little cafes that lined one side of the boulevard were full.

We wandered through the jumble of stalls, browsing books, vinyl records, and collectables. I picked up a pair of vintage shoes that looked like they dated from the 1940s.

'Five euros,' the stallholder said promptly. 'For that, you

can have both!'

I looked up sharply to see a mischievous grin and twinkly eyes. I laughed. Then it struck me. He had spoken in Portuguese but I had translated it automatically. And I had understood his joke! The little exchange, short though it was, felt like a breakthrough. Triumphantly, I went to find Geoff to tell him.

We grew to treasure the unexpected little discoveries the city offered, with their opportunities for interesting encounters. Shortly after our move we had wandered into the backstreets off Rua de Cedofeita. The hotel we had stayed in on our first trip to Portugal was on Cedofeita and we liked the area. One of the smaller streets running parallel to Cedofeita was full of antique shops, small grocery stores, and interesting cafes.

One warm evening, we were slowly making our way home after having a meal at a restaurant and found ourselves at the end of this street. We decided to stop at an unassuming cafe for coffee. Sitting at one of the outside tables, we got into conversation with a young Brazilian man who told us that (like many Portuguese people) he worked in the UK. He had just flown back home to Portugal after a few weeks away. He insisted on paying for our coffees. His young son, who was about ten, stared at us curiously and asked, 'Quanto anos tem?'

At the time, our Portuguese language skills were shaky and we could only offer a helpless 'Não compreendemos.'

Patiently, the boy repeated his question several times, getting louder each time, until he was actually shouting. His father managed to stop giggling long enough to translate for us. His son had simply been asking how old we were. When the boy learnt that we were in our forties, he raised his eyebrows and blew out his cheeks in awe at our advanced ages!

We arranged to meet our Brazilian friend the following night at the same cafe. However, when we arrived, the cafe owner told us that he had phoned to say he would be delayed. We waited a while but eventually had to leave as we had booked a table in a restaurant. But before we left, we slipped the cafe owner some money to return our friend's kindness and buy him a coffee.

In fact, we soon developed the habit of searching out interesting cafes in some of the quieter corners of the city. This is not a difficult task in Porto. If a person were so inclined, they could spend a day walking the streets of the city and be confident of finding a good cafe every few yards or so. You will never die of hunger or thirst in Porto. While we appreciated the decor and ambience of some of Porto's larger and more famous eateries, such as Café Majestic on Rua Santa Catarina, we had a sneaking affection for smaller, more down to earth establishments.

In Gaia, we found a tiny cafe near El Corte Inglés. Café Sol had the benefit of several tables set outside on a terrace and served the best coffee and cake we had ever tasted. Like many small businesses in Portugal it was family-owned and several members of the family worked in the cafe. In Porto, our favourite cafe was Café Tropical, a very traditional establishment near Rua Santa Catarina, but situated well off the main thoroughfare.

The cafe was long and narrow, with a long polished formica bar and 1950s-style bar stools down one side. If you managed to walk past the counter near the door and resist the fresh cakes, pastries, and bread displayed there, you would find yourself in a space that was not large but was crammed with small tables. At lunchtimes, the cafe was packed. If you were lucky enough to get a table, you were treated to a lively performance while you ate your lunch. The coffee machines behind the counter hissed, shouts and steam issued from the kitchens, which were visible through a large serving hatch, and waiters nipped rapidly through the narrow spaces between the tables, balancing precarious-looking trays. The food was always excellent and astonishingly cheap: at five euros for a three course meal with wine, eating out didn't have to feel like a rare luxury.

Cafe Tropical seemed to have lots of regular customers and we came to know several of them by sight. One of them, an elderly man, always had a book with him. Once he had settled himself at his table and opened his book, a waiter would appear with a glass of red wine and set it before the man, who would nod briefly. Then a bowl of soup would appear. This would be followed by a main course and a dessert. Finally, a small coffee would be placed in front of the reader. All of this would occur without a word passing between the man and the cafe staff. After finishing his *cafezinho*, the man would carefully stow away his book, slap some money on the table, and leave.

Eating out is much more popular in Portugal than in the UK, and it is common for people to spend a higher proportion of their income on going to cafes or restaurants. Often when we called at a cafe for a *lanche* and coffee at lunchtime, we would see elderly couples consuming large three course meals complete with wine. We would gaze at their heaped plates in awe, envious at their powers of digestion.

Perhaps the habit of eating well partly explained why many of the older folks we knew, like Beatriz, looked much younger than their years. We had assumed at first that Beatriz and António were in their sixties, but we later found out that Beatriz was seventy-two and António was nearly eighty. We knew that they always had a substantial cooked lunch and regularly met up with family or friends to eat at restaurants, despite being on pensions. They were obviously doing something right.

One of the joys of sitting outside a good cafe in warm weather is the opportunity it provides for people-watching. This was one of our favourite pastimes, and cost only the price of a drink. There is nothing like sitting at a pavement cafe over a beer or coffee and watching the life of the city whirl around you. And Porto is a city with both spirit and style. We would observe the chic young women hurrying past in impossible heels, the smart young men with their neat polo shirts and manicured beards, the gaggles of new university students slightly self-conscious in their long black gowns. But we liked to watch the older people the best.

In Portugal, many older people still dress quite formally. Of course, jeans and trainers have starting encroaching but we noticed that many older men still wore suit trousers, shirts, and jackets ... and very often waistcoats and hats too. One day in Porto, we observed an elderly man buying a newspaper from a *tabaco* stand (these little kiosks sell tobacco, newspapers, and other essentials). The man was wearing tailored trousers in deep purple, with a matching waistcoat. His shoes were polished to a high shine. A smart Mackintosh, pink tie, and purple hat completed the look. He was elegance personified.

Not to be outdone, older women are similarly careful about their dress. Some of the older widows still follow the traditional practice of wearing all black. However, leopard print — on scarfs, shoes, and coats — is popular in Portugal, and the extent to which it is worn is linked to age. It is almost *de rigueur* for many women of more advanced age, as is the use of shades of silver and gold.

On the bus to Foz do Douro one winter's day, we noticed a very elderly lady in a jaw-dropping outfit. She wore a leopard print coat with a black furry collar and a matching hat. Black leather trousers ended in gold ankle boots adorned with tassels. A silvery gold leather shoulder bag with a gold chain and numerous gold bangles completed the look.

The best thing about the woman's outfit was that nobody on the crowded bus looked twice at her. In the UK, that outfit (on any woman, regardless of her age) would be considered eccentric at best and rather vulgar at worst. We like the way that Portuguese society seems much more tolerant; the leopard print lady on the bus certainly attracted many glances but we noticed that they were interested and admiring rather than critical.

Perhaps the Portuguese climate has something to do with fashion choices. The strong sunlight and vivid blues of sky and water demand something stronger than sober shades and pastel hues. Like the intense whites and vivid colours of the houses, the vibrant clothes seem to reflect the atmosphere of this lively city and its people (who are known as *Portuenses*).

However, much as I liked the idea of eventually embracing animal print leggings and silver sandals, the transformation would have to wait. Negotiating the hills of Porto was difficult enough in sturdy trainers. Trudging up the hills in the Ribeira district we were often overtaken by wiry young men and women speeding past in shorts and flip-flops. It was hard to know whether well-developed calf muscles were an inbuilt trait of the Portuenses or whether they were acquired after a childhood negotiating the city streets. Either way, we didn't have their stamina or ankle strength. Shortly before their first trip over, we advised the Mums to bring stout shoes or trainers.

It is always nice, when one knows a place well, to experience it afresh through the eyes of newcomers. Neither of our mothers had visited Portugal before and they were as charmed with Porto as we were. They were gratifyingly wide-eyed at the foreignness of it all: the barges on the river, the sunny squares with their cobbles and fountains, the smell of *churrasqueira* and salt breezes, the old ladies with their stalls of embroidered linens and sizzling sardines under the statue of São João at the Ribeira.

We took them to the market we had visited with Beatriz, and to the much bigger open-air market that is held on Mondays at the seaside town of Espinho, a short train ride away. We lunched in one of the cafes on Espinho's tidy sea front, then strolled across the sand nibbling almond biscuits and strawberries bought from the market, and watching some of the locals surfing or lying on the beach slowly turning mahogany under the strong sun.

In Porto, we stumbled one morning into the little bird market that is held weekly in Campo dos Mártires da Pátria. Then, heads full of bird song, we took the Mums to see Mercado do Bolhão, the large historic market in the heart of Porto. The stalls of Mercado do Bolhão are arranged over two storeys in a beautiful neoclassical structure that dates from 1914. We browsed the covered stalls downstairs, admiring the displays of fruit and vegetables, the slabs of glistening fish, and the displays of fresh and dried flowers, and listening to the shouts of the stallholders.

Escaping up the wide stone steps to the second floor, it was a little quieter, and we gazed up at the blue blue sky. Before we left, we bought figs, olives, cheese, and bread rolls and picnicked on the grass by a fountain in a leafy square.

One hot afternoon, we wound our way through the steep alleyways that drop down from Sé to the Ribeira, admiring the tiny shrines set into the walls. You have to watch your footing on the steps as everywhere there is greenery to admire: plants cascading from balconies, colourful flowers spilling from pots set outside the little houses that line the alleyways. Near Sé, we discovered by chance the Museu de Arte Sacre hidden away down a back lane and took refuge in its cool rooms and tiny enclosed garden.

The Mums were bewitched by the river at night, when the lights of the houses and restaurants on the Ribeira are magically reflected in the glassy surface of the water. We took them down to the Cais de Gaia to view Porto from the opposite side of the river. We chose a small unassuming cafe on the *cais* where we struggled to ask for a pot of black tea, having frustratingly forgotten the word for 'black'.

Anxious to oblige, the cafe owner ushered us behind the counter to examine the different teas he had in stock, then taught us how to ask for black tea in Portuguese (*chá preto*). We sat outside the cafe with our tea and *pasteis de nata*, which the Mums had quickly developed a passion for, and gazed across the river at Porto, a many-layered jewel rising up from the river bank.

Despite the attractions of the city, our visitors also fell in love with the charms of our neighbourhood. Hospitable as ever, Beatriz and António invited them over for tea and Beatriz was thrilled at her two new English *amigas*. We took them up to meet Mrs Costa, and spent a happy morning in the bakery in the parish centre. And we did one of the things we liked best: sitting in the garden soaking up the sun, fussing with Bibby, and looking at the boats gliding past on the river.

One warm May evening, we decided to light up the charcoal barbecue we had bought from Senhor Pereira's. Geoff made some vegetarian burgers for us and we bought some fresh sardines for the Mums to try. We had salad leaves from the garden and a bottle of *vinho verde* purchased from Mrs Costa.

The barbecue was smoking away merrily when we heard loud shouting from across the lane. Quickly opening the gate, we saw Alta Man waving frantically and yelling 'Fogo! Fogo!'

'Não! No fire! Não fogo,' Geoff shouted back. 'Um … hell, what's the word for barbecue … I know, churrasco! Sardinhas!'

Alta Man looked puzzled for a moment then realization dawned. 'Sardinhas? Ahh ... muito saborosas!' He sniffed the air appreciatively.

We beckoned for him to come and join us, but he smiled and shook his head, looking slightly abashed.

'Do you think he was angling for an invite to sample the food?' I asked Geoff later.

'No ... I think he just didn't expect anyone to be having a barbecue in May. After, all, it is a chilly 20 degrees!'

11

Given our lack of income during our first couple of years in Portugal, it was a relief to have the garden finally producing some food. We were slowly turning our little plot into a kitchen garden. We planted a lime tree, three apple trees, and a pear. We also acquired some raspberries and lots of herbs. We sowed tomatoes, peppers, lots of salad leaves, and anything else we could get our hands on.

We had discovered two wonderful seed shops in Porto, both near Mercado do Bolhão. One was furnished with wooden floor-to-ceiling drawers and staffed by two elderly men, who dressed very properly in suits. Even a small purchase of one packet of seeds was slowly wrapped up in paper with the utmost care.

Beatriz looked at our lime tree with suspicion and then kindly donated some cuttings from the large bay and rosemary bushes in her own garden. Beatriz' main garden passions were roses and orchids; she had a large collection of the latter and fussed over them constantly. However, like many of our neighbours, she grew potatoes and the tall Portuguese cabbage. This is actually a variety of kale, and has the advantage of a long growing season; leaves can be picked from the long stems for many months.

In the lower garden we planted some alpine strawberries. We loved the sharp sweetness of their tiny fruit. Beatriz examined these one day and shook her head in pity.

'Demasiado pequenas,' she said, shaking her head; too small.

We tried to explain that there was nothing wrong with our strawberry plants: they were just a small variety. However, horticultural technicalities were beyond the scope of our limited Portuguese and I suspect Beatriz left with the impression that we were just useless at gardening.

We had the same reaction from Senhor Motta, another neighbour who lived opposite Beatriz. Motta (as he was known locally) occasionally passed our house to reach the little allotment he kept nearby. He was a large solid man with enormous bushy eyebrows that framed a square-shaped swarthy face. He spoke slowly, with a shy smile and many interjections of 'Graças a Deus', uttered with his eyes cast upwards to the heavens.

This pious attitude was not entirely in accord with Motta's activities. We had gleaned from Beatriz that Motta was quite the local entrepreneur. He was always involved in little bits of business and had fingers in many pies, few of which were totally legal. Motta considered the concepts of income tax, planning permission, and other niceties to be infringements to his basic human rights and ignored them as a point of honour.

We had mentioned to Beatriz that we were considering installing a wood-burning stove in the sitting room and she had recommended Motta to us. According to Beatriz' glowing account, Motta was a *trolha* (a labourer) but he was also a master craftsman and artisan. He had constructed a large fireplace for Beatriz and António and she was sure he would do a marvellous job of installing a stove for us. We had planned to ask Jorge, our builder, to do the job but as Motta was a neighbour and worked only itinerantly, it seemed only fair to direct some work his way.

When we broached the project with Motta, he was enthusiastic. He would come round, he said, to weigh up the site. He brought with him some large strawberry plants from his allotment; apparently, news of our sick strawberries had spread. He spent some time pointing out the large fruits on the plants he had brought, before asking where we intended to plant them. We told him that they would be going in the lower garden with their miniature cousins, because that part of the garden was the shadiest. He shook his head sadly.

'Sol, sol!' he insisted, and gestured to the garden bed outside the sitting room window.

We tried to explain that the soil in the top garden was very free-draining; this, together with the sun exposure, meant that plants in this part of the garden sometimes suffered in the summer. Motta laughed, brushing aside our concerns, and seized a trowel. Before we could stop him, he started digging a spot for the strawberries. Amused, we left him to it; they could always be moved later when he had gone.

After his spot of planting, Motta appraised the proposed site of the stove. Yes, it was a good position, he said. It would be *muito fácil* to install. He charged four euros an hour for his labour and he could take us in his car to look for a suitable stove the next day. We congratulated ourselves on taking Beatriz' advice; Motta seemed like the perfect man for the job.

The next day, Motta took us a local DIY store to buy a stove and the necessary flue pipe. We were to leave it all to him, he said. He was very experienced in this kind of work and knew exactly what we needed. The following day we went back to the store to exchange the flue pipe, Motta having discovered that he had chosen the wrong size. The day after that, we returned to exchange the fittings, and the day after that, we took both the pipe and fittings back because Motta had decided that the original size he had chosen was in fact correct.

And so it continued. We tried to help, but not being skilled artisans like Motta, common sense was all we could offer. Unfortunately, we discovered that Motta's standards for what constituted a good DIY job were generally at odds with our own. We were a little horrified, for instance, at his attempts to fit the flue pipe for the stove. He insisted that this should run up from the stove through the roof, despite us warning him that some of the new roof girders were metal, which would make the job difficult. We suggested running the flue pipe out through the wall. Undeterred, Motta cut a hole in the ceiling and then went up onto the roof with his hammer. After two hours of banging, he came down, sweating and dispirited, and announced that it would be much better to take the flue out horizontally through the wall. Relieved, we agreed, and tried not to think about what damage he had done to our roof.

Unsurprisingly, the new plan didn't go smoothly either. Once through the wall, the pipe had to run up the wall, angle outwards to avoid the gutter, and continue upwards for a couple of metres. Predictably, the fittings Motta had bought were not at the correct angle to achieve this. We were far from fussy, but when we saw Motta's first attempt we stared in disbelief. The pipe ran neatly up the wall to the gutter ... and then stuck out at a 45-degree angle. Motta was packing away his hammer, a satisfied look on his face.

'Fim!' he said triumphantly.

'It bloody well isn't finished,' said Geoff, and hurried inside to get a notepad and pen. When he showed Motta a sketch of how the pipe should look, Motta's face fell. Huffily, he got out his hammer and, with big sighs, repositioned the ladder.

We had started to realize that the hourly rate Motta charged for his work was not so economical as it seemed. Four euros an hour was cheap, unless of course the job ended up taking three months. We were beginning to think it might.

But finally the flue pipe was in. We asked Motta where he was planning to get the tiles from, to cover the part of the sitting room wall behind the stove. He looked at us blankly. When we pointed out that the wall would need some kind of protection from the stove he agreed enthusiastically. He had a solution, he said. And it would be much cheaper than tiles. Geoff and I exchanged worried glances.

Motta disappeared to the builders merchants, leaving us to fret about what he was up to. When he reappeared he was clutching a large bulky square object that looked like a bit like polystyrene wall insulation. One side was covered with silver foil.

'What is it?' I asked Geoff.

'I'm not sure ... but it looks worryingly like asbestos!'

Motta brandished his square proudly and then with elaborate care positioned it behind the stove so it was flush with the wall.

'Perfeito!' he said.

I looked at the ugly, possibly toxic silver square and shook my head.

'Não.'

Motta looked astonished. He explained that the square could be removed when the fire wasn't lit and then brought out again when it was needed. Easy!

'Não,' I said firmly.

Motta gave me a disbelieving smile then looked at Geoff and shrugged his shoulders, as if to say 'Women!'

We eventually agreed to disagree about Motta's Heath

Robinson solution, and he headed out to the car to return it to the builders merchants, no doubt muttering under his breath about the unreasonable fussiness of English women. Although the set-up was far from ideal, the stove worked for now.

The following year, we asked Jorge to come and redo the installation. A couple of years later, the top of the pipe that Jorge had installed fell down. We decided it was time to do the job properly. We exchanged the old stove, which was rusting badly, for a new one and bought some better quality flue pipe. Geoff fitted the stove and the pipe in a fraction of the time that Motta had taken. If Motta ever noticed that the system he had bodged had been replaced, he never said anything.

The wood stove was a welcome addition to the house. We had never imagined having to worry about being warm in Portugal, but the winters were getting colder. And Portuguese houses are not built for cold weather. The stone walls and tiled floors that kept our house cool in summer made for chilly winter evenings. Most houses in Portugal do not have central heating; the country has few natural gas resources and electricity is not particularly cheap. Because of our short staircase the heat from the new stove heated the whole house, and suitable logs were cheap and widely available.

Whether it was the cold weather or the remnants of the virus that had affected Geoff's eye in the UK, he started to feel unwell. This manifested as a general lack of energy, along with other, odder symptoms. He became very sensitive to light and began to get troublesome muscle aches and twitches. Appetite problems started to worsen into nausea and then vomiting.

We didn't know what to do. We weren't yet registered at the local health centre, and Geoff was unwilling to consult a doctor anyway.

'They'll just put it all down to high blood pressure,' he said. 'And it's more than that.'

He had been working very hard, trying to get the garden into some sort of shape and had also been working on two books, which were almost finished. We concluded that his symptoms might be an echo of the chronic fatigue he had suffered seven years ago, when we lived in the UK. Maybe he just needed to take it easy.

I gave him some acupuncture and massage, and he had some days when he wasn't too bad. But his condition declined. Beatriz had noticed that Geoff wasn't out and about in the garden much and she was concerned. She brought round treats; cakes, homemade fritters she called *iscas*. But Geoff's occasional cravings for certain types of food often quickly turned into lack of interest in food and stomach problems.

Beatriz urged us to visit the doctor. The trouble was, neither of us had any faith in the power of Western medicine to treat what seemed to be a flare-up of Geoff's original problem. Western medicine is better at dealing with structural problems than with energetic ones.

Then one night it all came to a head. Dozing in bed, Geoff experienced excruciating cramps in his calves, then passed out. I couldn't wake him. Panicked, I inserted an acupuncture needle into a point that is used to revive a person who has fainted. To my relief, he woke, but he was slurring his words and not fully aware. I phoned an ambulance.

After blood tests in the emergency department of the local hospital, Geoff was transferred to the nephrology ward. We were told that his kidneys were failing. I don't know if you are familiar with that sinking feeling of disbelief that occurs during a crisis, where life suddenly feels like it is happening to somebody else. It would not an exaggeration to say that everything changed for us with the news.

That night, and for several subsequent days, Geoff was placed on haemodialysis to clean the toxins that had accumulated in his blood. The nephrologist we spoke to declared his condition to be chronic.

'His kidneys have been damaged for a long time,' she said. 'Probably due to high blood pressure.'

But when we showed her the results of the blood tests Geoff had in the UK shortly before we moved, she looked thoughtful.

'This means it's more acute,' she said. 'That puts a very different light on the situation.'

There was a slim possibility that Geoff's kidneys would recover. But until they did, he would need regular dialysis. The hospital arranged for him to attend a dialysis clinic three times a week and put him on the waiting list for a kidney transplant that we hoped he wouldn't need.

One of the nephrology nurses at the hospital, Martim, spoke perfect English and was thrilled to learn that Geoff was a writer. He himself was writing a book and appeared one day with a sheaf of papers, which were the first two chapters of his book. He wanted Geoff to read them and provide feedback.

'It will give you something to do during dialysis!' he said.

But Geoff found the four-hour dialysis sessions a struggle. Lying in the same position for so long with only one arm free (the other was hooked up to the machine) was tiring and frustrating. Martim urged him to try ambulatory dialysis. This works via a catheter attached to the peritoneum and so can be performed at home, obviating the need for haemodialysis.

'It gives you more freedom,' Martim said. 'You can go

travelling and everything.'

'I don't want to go travelling,' Geoff replied. 'I'm knackered!'

But if it meant that Geoff could spend more time at home, the ambulatory method seemed worth a try, and he duly had the small operation to insert the necessary catheter. Unfortunately, before he could try home dialysis, he got appendicitis, probably as a result of the catheter surgery. After an appendectomy and another spell in hospital, he had had his fill of surgery. He decided to stick with the haemodialysis.

The hospital found a place for him at a dialysis clinic in Gaia city centre. Three evenings a week, he was picked up by the local volunteer fire and ambulance service and ferried to the clinic. The haemodialysis session lasted four hours, so by the time he was dropped back at home it was often after 11 pm and he was exhausted.

It is possible to become used to most things, however unpleasant. We soon fell into a new routine. With only one hand free, it was impossible to eat a proper evening meal at the clinic so Geoff would take two sandwiches made from *pão de água*, an airy but substantial type of bread, and also some homemade cake or biscuits. The clinic staff brought the patients coffee during the treatments.

At 5 pm the ambulance would career down the lane at an alarming speed. The driver in charge of the evening pick-up service was Diogo, a short rotund man with a loud voice and a raucous laugh. Diogo would leap out of the van and bellow a greeting, sliding back the ambulance door in his customary gung ho manner. Dona Mariana, a tiny frail lady in her 70s who attended the same dialysis clinic, would already be in the ambulance and Diogo would pick up various other people on the way. Once at the clinic, Geoff and Diogo would go for a coffee in the next door cafe, which helped to pass the forty minutes or so it took for the session to start.

Diogo often regaled Geoff with tales of the ghost that apparently inhabited the fire station building. Several of the staff had seen a mysterious figure in white, and many had heard strange noises, often at lonely hours of the night but also in the daytime. At first, Geoff attributed the tales to Diogo's story-telling capacity and tendency for embellishment. However, one evening, he got talking to the driver who was standing in for Diogo while he was on leave. Geoff happened to mention the ghost and the young man shuddered.

'I don't work there at night any more,' he said. 'I daren't. That's when the ghost appears!'

Once he got used to the sessions, Geoff started taking some work to the clinic with him. He would write, think ideas through, and read. But some music and a set of headphones were essential. The clinic could be a noisy place. Much of the noise was created by Big João, one of the other patients. Everything about Big João was oversized, from his large paunch to his bellowing laugh. Like Geoff, many of the patients took with them books, phones, laptops, or knitting to while away the time. But not João. He spent the evening talking at people, usually at the top of his voice.

One evening, Geoff recorded a sample of Big João's chatter on his phone and played it back to me over supper.

'Can you hear how loud he was?' Geoff asked me. 'He's deafening. I couldn't hear myself think!'

'Was he in the chair next to you then?'

'No! He was right across the room! He was next to Dona Mariana. She's probably deaf now.'

Big João was in constant conflict with the clinic nurses about his diet, but their attempts to persuade him to lose weight were unsuccessful. Geoff and Diogo would often see Big João at the cafe next to the clinic, downing a few beers before his dialysis session. João reasoned that just before a session was the perfect time to relax his fluid-restrictive diet and indulge in a blow-out! Many other patients had the same idea, and Geoff often saw people eating bananas (which are rich in potassium and so restricted for dialysis users) and other 'forbidden foods' with gusto just before their dialysis session.

Geoff had his own battles at the sessions. There were two nephrologists at the clinic. One was warm and friendly and had a good rapport with the patients. The other was distant and rather sour, and didn't appear to like her job very much. You can probably guess which one Geoff was assigned to.

Managing the health of people on haemodialysis usually involves close monitoring of fluid intake, body weight, and blood pressure. Although research shows that well-being and energy are important indicators of health, these factors are often neglected. Recent approaches highlight the importance of maintaining adequate weight, especially in older people. However, the relative importance placed on various aspects of health in nephrology can vary according to the doctor. Geoff's nephrologist believed that a low body weight and the blood pressure of a ten-year-old were ideal for people on dialysis.

Because of his academic background, Geoff was eager to read scientific journal articles about his condition, and his training in Chinese medicine meant that he was practiced in monitoring his own body. These tendencies were frowned upon by his nephrologist, who preferred her patients to be compliant rather than proactive.

'She hates me,' he complained one evening after another dispiriting encounter with his doctor, who he called

'Madam', a nickname that summed up her bossy attitude.

'She doesn't hate you,' I said. 'She's just not used to patients wanting to be involved in their own treatment.'

'She thinks I'm being obtuse,' Geoff said. 'You know what she said when I asked if my body weight could be increased?'

'What?'

'She told me that if I put more weight on I would explode!'

At 70 kg, Geoff was hardly fat. He was only just starting to recover from the muscle wastage he had experienced during his illness. His blood pressure was now so low he had no energy to do anything. One evening before he left for dialysis he declared that he was going to raise this with Madam, and ask her to reduce his medication.

'What did she say?' I asked when he came home that evening, worn out.

'Well, I told her that every time I stood up to cross the room I felt lightheaded.'

'And what did she say?'

'She told me not to stand up!'

It was hard to stand by and hear about Geoff's physical and psychological struggles at the clinic but there was little I could do. It seemed that some of Madam's other patients also found her draconian approach difficult. Little Dona Mariana was also one of Madam's patients and was frail as a sparrow. She often had low blood pressure episodes after dialysis and sometimes passed out in the back of the ambulance on the way home. Geoff always kept a close eye on her on the way home in case she had an episode *en route*.

One of the newer clinic patients caused rather more disruption. The ambulance now picked up another elderly lady, Dona Antónia, who was very chatty and friendly.

Unfortunately, she was also a little confused.

One evening, Geoff was very late home.

'What happened?' I asked.

'Well, we went to Dona Antónia's house to drop her off and Diogo took her to the front door. But then they came back and got back in the ambulance.'

'Was no-one in?'

'Oh yes. A woman answered the door. But it turned out that she was the new owner of the house. Dona Antónia moved out a year ago!'

Poor Dona Antónia. Haemodialysis is very taxing on the system and it is possible that her memory problems were a result of the treatment. Or perhaps she was beginning to experience symptoms of dementia. Either way, Dona Antónia's confusion could derail the return journey. And this was not the first time it had happened. Diogo was usually the driver for the evening shift and he soon became wise to Dona Antónia's misdirections. But if a different driver was standing in, chaos could ensue.

On one memorable evening, Geoff was two hours late getting home from the clinic. Dona Antónia had taken the driver to her old address, then had redirected him to another, even older, address, a house she had lived in over ten years ago! After that, Geoff had to be on the alert during every return journey if Dona Antónia started chatting to the driver. At the mention of any street names, Geoff would interject and tactfully redirect the driver.

'I should be on a salary,' Geoff said to me one evening on his return.

'What do you mean?'

'Well, tonight I had to give Dona Mariana a biscuit to stop her fainting, try to explain to Dona Antónia where she lives, and give the driver a quick English lesson!'

12

Ironically, one unexpected outcome of Geoff's illness was that it seemed to integrate us more firmly within our new community. Beatriz of course offered lots of support; she and her son had driven to the hospital to offer support on the night Geoff was taken in, and after he returned home she frequently called round with small gifts of food she had cooked.

But we were surprised by the concern shown by other neighbours. While Geoff was recuperating at home, I did the shopping and other errands alone. I was constantly getting stopped by people we didn't know, but who obviously knew us, and asked about Geoff's progress. One elderly lady who lived near Mrs Costa's shop always stopped when she saw me, put down her shopping bags, and gave me a big hug, before asking after Geoff.

I also had to give regular updates to Mrs Costa, the Pereiras from the hardware shop, and Maria and Lena. Alta Man stopped me on the lane one day to ask how Geoff was getting along with the evening dialysis sessions. I shouldn't really have been surprised that he knew that the sessions were in the evening. Alta Man's personal neighbourhood watch would ensure he knew exactly what time Geoff left in the ambulance and what time he returned home!

One summer evening, however, Alta Man was rather put out when the ambulance stopped outside his own house after picking up Geoff. It had been a hot, dry day, but Alta Man had decided to light a small bonfire to burn some garden cuttings. The volunteer fire service had been busy all summer dealing with wild fires, and although Alta Man was attending carefully to his blaze, the sight of a plume of smoke on that warm evening was too much for Diogo. He jumped out of the ambulance, raced over to the garden wall, and began to loudly harangue an indignant Alta Man about the dangers of forest fires.

One welcome result of this extra social interaction was that our Portuguese language skills began to improve. Although many doctors and nurses in Portugal speak excellent English, Geoff had had plenty of opportunities to hone his language skills during his hospital stay and during clinic visits. And some of the staff liked having an English patient to practice their own language skills on.

In the hospital one day, Júlia, one of the nurses, brought Geoff a cup of coffee and some biscuits. As she offered him the tray, she said in English, 'Are you angry?'

'What about?' Geoff asked, surprised.

'It is time for snack, so you must be angry.'

'Why should I be ... oh, do you mean *hungry*?'

She laughed. 'Yes, yes, hungry is what I mean!'

Júlia knew both words, but her dropped 'h' and pronunciation of 'u' as 'a' had confused them both. But at least Júlia could hold a conversation in English. Our Portuguese proficiency was perfectly adequate for simple situations, like ordering a meal in a cafe or shopping at Mrs Costa's. But we struggled to understand the rapid, accented dialogue of the locals and found it hard to engage in more personal or complicated exchanges.

For example, Mrs Costa told us one day that Senhora Pereira had broken her leg. We decided to call in at the hardware shop on the way home and ask after her. We were surprised to see that rather than taking it easy, Senhora Pereira was seated in a chair behind the counter with her leg, which was in a heavy cast, propped on a footstool. Despite our protestations she struggled to her feet with the aid of crutches. She had to look after the shop, she said. Senhor Pereira was working at the other shop they owned, which was in Porto.

Our enquiries after her health prompted a long and involved account of (as far as we could tell) how she had broken her leg, exactly what the consultant had said, and the results of all the x-rays and scans she had had.

The combination of Senhora Pereira's rapid fire delivery and the plethora of unfamiliar medical terminology left us having to guess at which points to express sympathy, surprise, or amusement. It was exhausting.

We found Beatriz the easiest person to understand. She tended to speak slowly (unless she was annoyed, when she spit her words out like machine gun fire). She also enunciated very clearly and used expressive (and often comical) gestures and mimes to get her point across, so we could usually understand most of what she said.

And with more practice, our vocabulary was slowly increasing. However, a little knowledge can be a dangerous thing. Our growing confidence in starting conversations meant that mistakes, often embarrassing ones, were inevitable.

One morning, I was chatting to Beatriz' husband António on their balcony. He was telling me of the hobbies he had developed since his retirement a few years earlier. We had noticed that a popular hobby of many of the older men in our neighbourhood was keeping racing pigeons, so I decided to ask António if he liked pigeons.

'Gosta dos bombeiros?'

António looked at me with a startled expression.

'Diga?'

I repeated my question, pleased with myself for managing to string a simple sentence together.

'Gosta dos bombeiros?'

António raised his eyebrows, cleared his throat, and rapidly changed the subject.

Later that day, puzzled at António's odd reaction to my simple question, I consulted our Portuguese dictionary. To my horror, I discovered that the word for pigeons was 'pombos' not 'bombeiros'. What I had actually asked António was 'Do you like firemen?' No wonder he had been startled.

The hospital had advised us that we needed to register to ensure we were eligible to use Portugal's free national health service. I booked an appointment with the local Segurança Social office. I contemplated trying my bluff my way through the meeting with my nascent language skills but then thought better of it. One of my mother's friends, Liliana, was Portuguese and had offered her help if we ever needed it. Unfortunately, she lived in the UK. However, she kindly offered to be available by phone during the Segurança Social meeting.

Many officials in Portugal speak more than one language but some do not. The Segurança Social official I met was very friendly and apologized for not speaking English. She deliberately spoke slowly and clearly to help me understand her. However, a couple of minutes into the meeting I knew I was out of my depth. There was lots of unfamiliar terminology and no time to look up all the words in my dictionary. Luckily, Liliana was on hand. I passed my phone to the official and she conversed happily and rapidly with Liliana, who then translated for me. Her help was a lifesaver and meant that our registration went without a hitch.

Being an *estrangeiro* in a foreign land and not being fluent in the language can be daunting. You are an outsider in many ways. There is something exciting about this; in some ways, we liked being on the margins looking into our adopted community. As introverts, we preferred being slightly inaccessible. We enjoyed interacting with Beatriz and António and our other neighbours but we needed time on our own to write and think. We still felt the thrill of the unfamiliar when we heard spoken Portuguese and saw words and accents that still seemed strange on billboards and shop fronts. I loved collecting quirky brand names, deliciously odd because they were unfamiliar, like *Bimbo* bread, *Skip* laundry powder, and the wonderfully named washing-up liquid *Superpop*.

However, it is true to say that language offers a window onto the worldview of a people. Our growing understanding of the various expressions and colloquialisms used by our neighbours provided insights into their experience. The frequent use of *tem que ser* (it has to be) and *é vida* (that's life) illustrated a stoic, rather philosophical approach to life's trials and tribulations that we admired. We also liked the way that many people we knew showed a strong sense of self-reliance and a tendency to frugality.

We wondered whether these attitudes reflected a society that still carried the legacy of the authoritarian regime instituted by the dictator António de Oliveira Salazar in 1933. Salazar was overthrown in the peaceful 'Carnation Revolution' of 1974, but many older people still remember the difficulties experienced under Salazar. We sensed in the older neighbours in particular a strength of character and an ability for coping with hardships unfamiliar to many of us living through easier times.

For instance, we liked to chat to one of the older ladies who used the *lavadouro*. She lived a few lanes away, up a steep hill. Several times a week, she walked down to the *lavadouro* to do her laundry. We had also seen her washing her pots and pans in the spring, and then walking back up the hill carrying a big bag of laundry and an even bigger bag of dishes and pans. As she was very short, she could hardly be seen under her enormous load.

One day, I went down to collect water and found her washing her saucepans. She told me cheerily that although she had a sink in her kitchen at home, she wasn't tall enough to reach it easily. I suggested that some kind of footstool might help but laughing, she brushed away the idea. She was eighty-three, she said, and fit as a fiddle. She preferred to do all her washing at the spring. She told me that when she was young she used to work at the Mercado do Bolhão in Porto. Each day she would walk down the hill to the riverside on Gaia side, catch a boat over to Porto, then walk up the hill to the market. Each evening she would do the return journey. Even for a young person, that would have been a punishingly tough journey. No wonder that, at eighty-three, she was probably fitter than me and remarkably sanguine at what would normally be considered a lifestyle totally unsuitable for an octogenarian.

Several studies on personality and psychology have highlighted interesting similarities and differences between cultures. When cluster analysis, a type of analysis that identifies similarities between data sets, is used to analyse personality ratings, it shows that Portuguese people cluster with those from mainland China. Maybe this reflects the fact that both countries have experienced life under more authoritarian regimes.

When he was in hospital, Geoff got chatting to a Chinese

nephrologist who was interested in research. When he told her about the findings of these studies, he was surprised at her reaction.

'Oh no!' Dr Inês said. 'We Portuguese are nothing like the Chinese!'

Having lived in Portugal for many years, she felt she had integrated fully into Portuguese society and now had little in common with Chinese culture and sensibilities.

In many ways, Portugal reminded us of the UK in the 1950s. The country is not wealthy and many people, like the little *lavadouro* lady, have lifestyles characterized by few luxuries and much physical labour. In our neighbourhood at least, many of the older ladies spent the whole day in their aprons, cooking, cleaning the house, sweeping the paths outside the house, washing clothes down at the *lavadouro*, and waiting on the lane for morning visits of the bread and fish vans, which brought fresh produce daily.

Many of our neighbours did not have cars, which are expensive in Portugal. Those that did usually had very old cars, which, to judge by the way they sounded, seemed to run on little more than the grace of God. Motta's car was particularly ancient; we always knew it was him passing the house because the car made a sound like a sack of spanners and belched evil-smelling smoke when it went round a corner.

As far as we could tell, life for older Portuguese men was rather more relaxed. Like António, many men met up each day in the cafes or in the little squares, where they sat and played cards, smoked, and spat, spitting being considered (as in China) a healthy way to rid the body of phlegm.

Our next door neighbour was an enthusiastic and accomplished spitter, and could often be heard as he strolled down the lane with his little dog, Fofo. Like most of the men in the neighbourhood, he was called António, so between ourselves, we called him The Man with the Dog. He was a reserved sort of chap, but kindly. The first time I had really talked to him, I was waiting for a bus to the hospital to visit Geoff. He too was travelling into town and went out of his way to explain where to catch the connecting bus to the hospital. He even accompanied me to the correct stop, waited with me until the bus came, and asked the driver to tell me where to alight.

The Man with the Dog was a widower. When he wasn't out on one of his frequent walks with Fofo, he tended to his pigeons. We often heard him shouting across to his friend João, a fellow pigeon fancier whose garden backed onto The Man with the Dog's. They had frequent long conversations about their precious birds, always conducted at shouting pitch.

We had become acquainted with João through Beatriz. She had gazed at our metal gate one day and frowned. There was a gap, she said, between the gate and the frame. We agreed that there was; the gate was old and the metal was slightly bent out of shape. Nevertheless the gate and the lock both worked fine. Beatriz disagreed. It was a security risk, she insisted. You never knew who would be prowling around. She glanced suspiciously up and down the lane, as if there were potential intruders lurking round every corner.

We were amused. We both felt this was one of the safest places we had ever lived. We felt perfectly safe walking round Gaia and Porto, even at night. In the UK we had often felt we had to watch our backs in the city at night. Here, it felt different. We liked the way that at the station or in a hospital waiting room, for instance, you could leave your bag on a seat if you wanted to pop to the toilet and no-one would dream of taking it. Moreover, you knew that other people would keep an eye on your property and respond if there was any trouble.

We therefore took Beatriz' rather dramatic warnings with a large pinch of salt. Her own behaviour belied her concerns; if she was popping round to our house she would leave her front door unlocked even if António was out. Anyway, any suspicious characters hanging round the neighbourhood would quickly be noticed thanks to Beatriz' and Alta Man's gossip grapevine.

However, to reassure Beatriz, we agreed with her suggestion to employ João to fix our gate. Apparently, he had a small home workshop where he did metalwork and a little carpentry. Like Motta, João did odd jobs in the neighbourhood. Although we had had our fingers burnt with Motta's handiwork, fixing the gate was a small job and, we hoped, would prove less of a disaster than the stove. In fact, João did an efficient and professional job and refused to accept anything more than three euros for his work.

Several of our neighbours did little bits of itinerant work in the area. The house two doors down from Beatriz contained a makeshift vehicle repair workshop that specialized in motorcycles. We called its owner Malcolm, after the character in the British television sitcom *Watching*. In the series, Malcolm repairs motorcycles from his mother's garage, frequently disrupting the neighbourhood with the noise and smell of the bikes he works on. Similarly, our local Malcolm tested out his bikes by racing up and down the lane at speed, and annoyed Beatriz by noisily revving the engines in his workshop.

The house a few doors down from Baixa Man had a large terraced plot and Geoff often saw the man who lived there, who was about seventy, working in his garden. We thought we had heard Beatriz refer to this neighbour as Manuel but when we called him this one day, she corrected us; he was Not Manuel, she said, he was another João. But after that conversation he became forever known to us as Not Manuel.

As Geoff slowly regained his strength he started to get the garden into shape. He cut down the old orange tree, which had died, and planted a fig tree and a new orange tree in the large pots we had bought from Senhor Pereira. He moved some of the bulbs that we had found in the garden to pots, and planted garlic, onion sets, and potatoes. If Geoff was working in the garden, Not Manuel would wave and start a conversation. Unfortunately, he was a little deaf so any exchange involved a lot of shouting and gesturing.

Not Manuel grew cabbages, marrows, tomatoes, and beans in his garden. He did all the work himself and it was a labour of love. The large garden was on two levels. Not Manuel grew all his vegetables on the top level, which was kept neat and free of weeds. However, this level was partly bordered by a high wall, which was smothered every year by pellitory, a pretty but invasive plant, much to the distress of Not Manuel.

To add to the work, the lower garden, which contained only a large fig tree, was also full of weeds by the end of summer. Every year, as soon as the weather started to warm up in February, Not Manuel would take his hoe (the gardening tool of choice in Portugal) and do battle. He would spend almost all day in the garden, cigarette dangling from his lips. First he would scrape all the pellitory off the wall. Then he would tackle the lower garden. By April, after several weeks of toil, he would stand proudly gazing at the bare earth in the lower garden and at his clean wall. Unfortunately, by autumn, all the weeds would be back and Not Manuel would have to start again the following year.

Every summer we traded produce with Not Manuel; he

would bring round a couple of huge marrows, or some cucumbers or lemons, and we would give him some tomatoes or physalis fruit.

Like Beatriz, Not Manuel was suspicious of any foods he was unfamiliar with. Wandering round our garden one day, he gazed with astonishment at the sweet cherry tomatoes we were growing and asked Geoff what was wrong with them. Geoff tried to explain that they weren't stunted; they were just a different variety. One day, Geoff offered Not Manuel some peas straight from the pod. Not Manuel backed away hurriedly, looking slightly panicked, and protesting that they weren't cooked! Nothing we said could persuade him to try a pea.

We had often encountered this conservative attitude to food and cooking. We tried to give Alta Man some limes one day. He looked at them suspiciously. What was wrong with our lemons? he asked. Why weren't they ripening? We weren't surprised that he was unfamiliar with this particular fruit. It is lemons rather than limes that feature in Portuguese cooking. Once, we took some home-grown courgettes round to Beatriz'. We knew that she made fresh soup every day and *abobora*, pumpkin, was one of the main ingredients. The courgettes would make a nice change.

Beatriz seemed pleased with the courgettes but when we suggested she could use them in her soups she shook her head.

'Uso abóbora,' she said.

In vain did we try and persuade her that courgettes were in the same family as pumpkins and could be used as a substitute.

She shook her head stubbornly and repeated 'Abóbora.'

No doubt she did cook and eat the courgettes but I doubt if they went anywhere near her soup pot.

This conservative attitude to food is understandable;

the national cuisine of Portugal is fantastic and people are proud of their traditional and local dishes. But of course, everyone knows the very best recipe for a particular dish and will fiercely debate any deviation from it.

When Geoff was in hospital, the patient in the bed opposite was a man called Tomás. Frail and elderly, Tomás slept most of the day, waking only for his meals. However, on the 24th June, the feast of São João, the patients were served sardines, which are traditionally eaten on this holiday. Tomás came to life. He ate his meal with relish, then spent the rest of the afternoon vociferously complaining about the way the *sardinhas* had been cooked, and about the fact that they had been served with *arroz* (rice). Sardines should always be served with potatoes and olive oil, Tomás insisted. He spent the whole afternoon loudly lecturing the ward about this fact with the mantra, 'Sardinhas, batatas com azeite!'

As a fish dish, the popularity of *sardinhas* is matched only by that of *bacalhau*, which is sometimes cooked in beer. We were shopping at Mrs Costa's one day when a local man stumbled into the shop. His wife was cooking *bacalhau* he said, and they had run out of beer. Judging by the man's gait, it was fairly obvious where all the beer had gone!

Beatriz of course had her own favourite recipe for the dish, which had been handed down to her by her mother. She made wonderful *bolinhos de bacalhau* (delicious little round fishcakes) and sometimes brought some round for us. We had started eating fish and a little meat after Geoff's illness. It is difficult for dialysis patients to consume enough protein, and some beans and legumes are restricted. It seemed easier to stick to the kind of diet Geoff had received in hospital, which included fish and meat.

Our new diet made it easier to buy food if we were out

and about. Portuguese cuisine showcases meat and fish, so sometimes it can be difficult to track down interesting meat-free options. Ham in particular is often added to everything. We bought freshly made 'vegetarian' egg salad baguettes one lunchtime from Espinho market. The baguettes were crammed with egg, grated carrot, cheese, and a wide range of other salad ingredients. They also had a good helping of ham, just to be sure! We felt it was pointless to complain; sliced ham is so ubiquitous we suspect some people count it as a type of vegetable.

Beatriz approved of our new non-veggie diet. She declared, often, that after his illness Geoff needed building up. Accordingly she frequently popped round with tasty morsels for him *arroz* with chicken, *iscas de bacalhau*, and (these he dreaded) huge pork chops. It was very sweet of her. Each time she brought something round, she would stand and patiently reel off the correct recipe for what she had cooked so that I could reproduce it. We had told her countless times that Geoff was the cook in our household but I don't think she believed us.

I had of course taken over the cooking when Geoff was ill and recuperating but once he was back on his feet he resumed kitchen duties. One day, I went down to the spring to collect water and bumped into Alta Man, who was filling his own water bottles. He asked after Geoff and I told him that my husband was doing well and was at that moment at home baking a cake. He looked astonished.

'Ele está a cozinhar?' he asked incredulously.

I nodded, then told him that Geoff did all the cooking. He shook his head slowly and smiled in wonder, as if I had just revealed to him a brand new law of the universe. And I suppose I had. For someone of Alta Man's generation, a world where men, rather than women, did all the cooking was a brave new world indeed.

13

At the time Geoff got ill we had just about run out of money. We had lasted almost two years on savings of about twenty-five thousand euros, which wasn't bad. But now very little of that was left. Geoff had published two non-fiction books and a novel. I had published one non-fiction book and had a completed novel that I still wasn't happy with and so was unlikely to see the light of day. Our publishing income was little more than a trickle. We didn't know then what we know now: unless you happen to write a blockbuster, it is very difficult to make a living from writing books. Our writing and scholarly interests were, and always had been, fairly niche. Our books were never going to be bestsellers. But we weren't prepared to sell our souls and write about areas we weren't interested in just to make a quick buck. Anyway, we were ex-academics; we were used to writing stuff that hardly anyone read!

I began to search for work that made use of my experience writing and eventually managed to find some online work copyediting. However, dialysis made it difficult for Geoff to work outside the home or to do any kind of online work that involved schedules. Not only did he have to fit in clinic visits, the day following dialysis he was always very tired.

Some days he was better than others, but it was difficult to predict his energy fluctuations. Working in the garden and cooking were therefore tasks that suited him, as he could fit them around how he felt.

So our lifestyle became in some ways similar to that of our neighbours. We had several sources of income, all rather small: the books, the editing, and the food we produced from the garden. Like our neighbours, we tried to grow as much as possible, both to save money and to ensure that we had fresh organic food. Unlike our neighbours, however, we kept no livestock. Motta kept rabbits for food and Alta Man kept chickens and turkeys in his large garden.

Baixa Man had died at a ripe old age and one of Motta's friends bought his little shack and the house next door to it and had them renovated. Until we got to know them, we called the new family (which consisted of a couple and their adult son) the Novos (the new people). They were about our age and very chatty. Nova Lady was a frequent user of the *lavadouro* and I often saw her down at the spring collecting water. Novo Man was less energetic. Once a day, he wandered listlessly into the garden to check his pride and joy: a motley collection of chickens. These scrappy looking creatures lived in a tumbledown hen house that Novo Man had built himself (although 'built' is perhaps too robust a word for the jumble of old bits of wood and corrugated iron that he had thrown together).

Nova Lady preferred cats to chickens, and enthusiastically took in all waifs and strays. Novo Man's chickens therefore shared the garden with an ever-growing gaggle of his wife's cats and their respective kittens. The kittens stomped on the roof of the chicken shack, stalked the hens, who chased them off vigorously, and generally made a nuisance of themselves. When the new chicks hatched, Novo Man had to make extra sure the chicken house door was secure, as both cats and kittens would sit outside longingly, pushing their noses against the mesh walls.

The eggs and meat from the chickens were no doubt a useful supplement to the diet of Novo People. Unfortunately for us, Novo Man bred his own chickens so there was always a cockerel amongst the group. I don't know how he did it, but Novo Man always managed to breed the most awful-sounding cockerel. This animal would strut about their garden giving off strange strangulated calls at the crack of dawn and thus waking everyone in the immediate neighbourhood. Everyone, that is, except Novo Man, who never rose before noon.

Several houses on our hill kept cockerels, though Novo Man's was the closest to our house. Once his cockerel had started its morning screech all the other cockerels in the neighbourhood joined in. The only relief from the daily chorus was in midwinter when all the cockerels seemed to disappear (presumably into various cooking pots) and the sun could rise in peace. In spring, the new generation of cockerels would take over and it would all begin again.

The rooster is a national symbol of Portugal, so it is maybe no surprise that the birds are popular, representing as they do a love of life. We sometimes speculated about the density of cockerels per square mile in Portugal. Whatever it is, we reckoned that our neighbourhood was well above the average. But the noise from Novo Man's chucks was as nothing compared to that issuing from the largest smallholding in the neighbourhood. This was situated further up the hill and was visible — and audible — from our garden. Old MacDonald, as we called him, kept chickens, geese, and ducks. Their quacking and cackling was particularly loud at feeding time, when Old MacDonald's two dogs usually contributed to the cacophony by barking senselessly.

One Christmas Eve morning we went outside to find a large duck on our kitchen roof. It didn't appear injured and had settled itself in a corner near the skylight to bask in the sun. Beatriz had spotted it from her balcony and came round to take a look. She told us that it was a sign of good luck to have a duck land on your roof on Christmas Eve. Though not, apparently, for the duck: Beatriz licked her lips and looked thoughtful. She was sure she had a good recipe for duck somewhere ...

At that moment, the doorbell rang. It was Old MacDonald who, like Beatriz, had spied the duck from his vantage point further up the hill. He must have read Beatriz' thoughts, for although his manner was friendly he looked at us a little suspiciously. The duck, perhaps having an inkling of the fate that awaited it, was reluctant to move and had obviously planned to stowaway on our roof for as long as it could. Maybe it somehow knew that we were the only vegetarians in the area. But to show Old MacDonald that we were no poachers, we helped him to shoo the creature off the roof and into the basket he had brought with him.

Even if we had wanted to keep some animals, our plot wasn't really big enough. Besides, it was Bibby's domain. Bibby had settled in well and was enjoying being master of all he surveyed. Our little garden wasn't exactly the forty acres he had enjoyed when we lived in Snowdonia, but we thought it plenty big enough for him. Bibby didn't agree.

With his mind on broader horizons, he patrolled the borders of the garden looking for any possible means of getting through the fence or over the wall. Then he hit upon a solution. By jumping onto the small wall that surrounded the patio, he found he could climb onto the kitchen roof, which was quite low. From here, he could survey the street and, a bit like Alta Man, keep a beady eye on all that was happening in the neighbourhood. We weren't too worried about this. After all, if he was on the roof, we knew where he was. And he seemed content to sit up there peering down on the street cats and dozing in the sunshine.

However, it wasn't long before Bibby noticed The Ledge. On the opposite side of the lane, the land sloped up to form a low flat ledge. This was the local stray cat feeding station. In Portugal, every neighbourhood has one, and they are usually maintained by the older ladies in the area. Beatriz was the boss of our Ledge, and had furnished it with a motley collection of old plates, bowls, and plastic trays. These were filled regularly by Beatriz and the other women of the neighbourhood.

It is a fact that many cats in Portugal often have a fondness for foods that are not commonly part of the feline diet, such as spaghetti, *piri piri* sauce, grated carrot, and cake. This is because they are often fed meal scraps as well as, or instead of, commercial cat food, which is rather expensive. The Ledge cats were occasionally given cat biscuits, but they usually had to be satisfied with scraps of fish and whatever leftovers were available. Beatriz had a liking for pasta, so the cats were connoisseurs of macaroni cheese, spicy spaghetti, and lasagne with meaty sauce.

The Ledge was frequented by an ever-changing cast of feline characters. Four different feline lineages dominated the neighbourhood: a line of stocky ginger cats, the jet black ones, the tabbies, and a family of large white cats with black smudges. In the early years, the main visitor to The Ledge was a huge ginger cat, who we called Laranja (which means orange). Beatriz insisted his colouring was more yellowy so she always called him Amarelo. He could be seen waiting patiently every morning for his breakfast spaghetti. Most of the gingers lived not far from Old MacDonald's, at the top of the hill, where there was another little feeding station. We suspected that Laranja was a member of this little group but had migrated down the hill to find his own territory.

Another dominant visitor was a cat who we nicknamed (rather literally) Tripod. He was a slim black cat with a friendly nature and only three legs. We were never sure if this was a birth defect or whether he was an amputee, which suggested that he was probably owned. If he was, he seemed happier to spend his days on the street. Despite his disability, Tripod was one of the most active cats in the neighbourhood and could often be seen walking precariously along the top of narrow walls, or climbing hazardously onto someone's roof. But it was in the mating season that Tripod most obviously displayed his astonishing energy. For weeks, he would limp through the lanes and gardens, courting the female cats until he called himself hoarse.

Some of the visitors to The Ledge were not strays at all. Two such were stocky little tabby females who belonged to Mariazinha, Alta Man's daughter. Beatriz resented the presence of these two on the grounds that they were not true strays and because they were Mariazinha's. Although Mariazinha was António's cousin, Beatriz didn't like her. She insisted that Mariazinha didn't look after her cats properly. In her turn, Mariazinha disapproved of Beatriz feeding the street cats. We thought that both women were alike in many ways, which probably explained why they didn't get on.

The constant display of food scraps on The Ledge was irresistible to Bibby. From his vantage point on the roof he soon learnt to spy on Beatriz when she came to deposit food for Laranja and Co. One day, Bibby disappeared. He wasn't on the roof and we couldn't find him anywhere in the garden. We eventually found him on The Ledge, scoffing scraps of food that, had we offered them to him in the kitchen, he would have turned his nose up at. He must have jumped down from the roof and trotted across the lane to investigate. This was a worrying development but unless we locked him in the house we couldn't really stop him.

Predictably, it wasn't long before Bibby's illicit wanderings got him into trouble. Jumping down awkwardly one day, he managed to injure his leg and had to be taken to the vet. At least the little plaster cast he was forced to wear for several weeks temporarily put paid to his nefarious activities. However, once recovered, he was up to his old tricks again, and even started sneaking into Alta Man's garden to steal cat biscuits. One day, I went to fetch Bibby, having spied him curled contentedly dozing under a bush, no doubt full of stolen food. Alta Man waved away my apologies. He liked Bibby, he said, and he didn't cause any trouble. And Mariazinha had taken a liking to him and often admired his beautiful colouring.

We were never sure how many cats Mariazinha had and we suspect that she wasn't either. Certainly, she always seemed to be losing one cat or another. Alta Man's garden was home to a constantly changing cast of felines, and Mariazinha was forever trekking down the lane calling after one cat or another. Sometimes she rang our bell to ask if we had seen Cat Such-and-Such. If she did spy one of her cats on The Ledge and called it, it would studiously ignore her. If she tried to catch it would usually run the other way. Bibby, in contrast, would always come to us when called; sometimes not immediately and not necessarily with a good grace if he didn't want to come, but he was much more responsive than Mariazinha's cats.

We had observed this rather distant attitude to cats amongst our neighbours. They fed and cared for the cats but rarely interacted with them or handled them. And they were never allowed in the house. Dogs, in contrast, are often treated like small children. The Man with the Dog doted on Fofo, and during their walks would keep up an affectionate running commentary to the dog.

However, we noticed that owner–dog relationships were often paradoxical. Although doted on and often spoilt, many owners let their dogs out each day to run around the neighbourhood. There was always a small gang of local dogs taking their morning constitutional, which usually involved gambolling down the lane and checking if there was any food on The Ledge. These dogs all seemed well-fed and well-cared for. In fact, one little black poodle who was part of the dog gang was expertly groomed and unless the weather was hot, did his daily patrols dressed in a little dog coat. His wardrobe must have been enormous because every time we saw him he had a different little coat on.

When I mentioned this practice to my mother, who was born in the 1940s, she wasn't surprised. She told me that when she was a girl, it was common practice to let your dog roam the streets for a few hours each day. One evening when Geoff was waiting outside the clinic for António, he saw a huge mastiff lope up the road. The clinic was situated on Avenida da República, the busy main street in the centre of Gaia. Geoff assumed the dog was lost, out on his own so late at night. However, the animal trotted purposefully up to a block of flats, stood outside the front door, and barked. Presently, a man came to the door dressed in pyjamas and took him in. The dog had simply been out for an evening stroll!

The dog gang that roamed our neighbourhood was generally peaceable and rarely bothered the cats. In fact, the larger cats like Laranja tended to bully some of the smaller dogs, who had to be mindful of a thwack from a large paw if they came to steal food from The Ledge.

Two of the most impressive cats in the neighbourhood were owned by Alta Man. These two were part of the patchy white cat line and were the size of small dogs. They usually stayed in Alta Man's garden but would occasionally stalk impressively down the lane, scaring all the other cats with their presence. One day, we were sitting on the patio when we heard a faint mewling sound from the other side of our wall. Geoff went out onto the lane to investigate. A few moments later he called me to come and look.

There, in a small cardboard box that had been placed in the shade of a lamp post, were two tiny kittens. One was white with black patches and the other was almost pure white with just a smudge of grey here and there. They looked for all the world like mini versions of Alta Man's white bruisers. They were immediately below his garden and so if they belonged to one of his white cats, they could conceivably have just fallen onto the lane. However, the way they had been placed in a box in a sheltered corner suggested not. We decided to call on Alta Man and see if he knew anything about them.

We found him in his garden staring at his lettuces. No, he said, he knew nothing about any kittens and would we like some onions? We asked whether either of his two white cats, both of whom were female, had been pregnant. No, no, not possible! he insisted. He gave them both contraceptive tablets he had obtained from the vet. What about Mariazinha? Might she know something about the kittens? Alas, said Alta Man, his daughter was at the hairdressers so he was unable to ask her. Now, were we sure we didn't want any onions?

We weren't entirely convinced by Alta Man's assurances but it was possible that the kittens had come from further afield. It was equally likely that Mariazinha knew something about them, but she was vague about her many cats at the best of times. We therefore gave up trying to establish where the kittens had come from and adopted them.

Twink and Dink, as we called them, were as disruptive to the household as kittens usually are, but they settled in well. Bibby was mildly surprised at their sudden appearance but tolerated them with little fuss. He spent most of his days on the roof anyway, and they were too small to follow him. They initially slept in the dining room at night, which we had cleared of anything breakable. After a few weeks, we reclaimed the room and they spent their nights in the *marquise*, the little porch-like room off the kitchen.

By then, one of the kittens seemed to have prematurely reached puberty. To our horror, Dink's raging hormones turned her into a little sex monster. Desperate to escape the *marquise* at night and find a mate, she literally climbed the walls, trying to find any means of escape. Unfortunately, the *marquise* was not a well-built structure and there were a few small gaps between the top of the windows and the sloping roof. Into these spaces Dink squeezed her tiny body, squealing and moaning with frustrated desire. We could hear her from the bedroom and several times a night she had to be extracted and calmed down. Every time we thought we'd filled all possible gaps, Dink managed to find another one.

Although Twink was calmer than her sister, she had her own particular talent for mischief. Twink was a climber, and nothing was out of bounds: shelves, the wardrobe, the curtains, and, when the kittens started to spend time in the garden, the roof. Although she was still too small to access the roof using Bibby's method she tried every other means, balancing on step-ladders and plant pots to try and reach high enough. Bibby would stare down at her efforts, a smug look on his face.

Twink also had a liking for holes and gaps, a dangerous streak of curiosity that we tried unsuccessfully to curb. If you dug a hole in the garden to plant something, Twink would stick her head in it. If you left any kind of empty container lying around, such as a paint pot, Twink's nose would be in it in seconds. She managed to ferret out all the tiny gaps in the fence that surrounded the steep part of the garden and worm her way through them. To stop her flinging herself off the terrace Geoff had to weave small pieces of chicken wire into the fence to try and make it Twink-proof.

'It's like bloody Colditz,' he complained one day. 'What's wrong with that cat?'

Never again, we vowed. No more kittens. But we were heartbroken when Dink disappeared one night. As they had grown, both cats had eventually managed to follow Bibby onto the roof each day. Bibby, older and lazier than the kittens, now usually contented himself with snoozing most of the day, keeping one eye open for any interesting happenings in the lane. But Twink and Dink were young and fearless. They didn't want to snooze; they wanted fun. They therefore started jumping down into the lane every day to accost Beatriz or bother the other cats. Afraid that one of them would bust a leg like Bibby, we decided the safest option was just to open the gate for them each morning and let them spend some time on the lane to satisfy their curiosity. For a few days, this worked well and then Dink just disappeared. Despite our searching we never found her. However, Twink soon had another small companion.

A constant danger for the stray cats that visited The Ledge were the cars. Our lane was not very busy, but a cat that wasn't streetwise or was half-asleep could come to grief, especially at night. One morning, we heard crying from The Ledge. It was coming from a young cat we had often seen in the lane. She was the offspring of one of the tabbies, and though no longer a kitten, was a small skinny little thing. We had given her the imaginative name of Kitty. She was on The Ledge but seemed to be in some distress. I went over to investigate. The poor little thing was damp and her fur was matted and bloody, particularly around her face. She had obviously been hit by a car.

We managed to get her into a cat box and took her to the vet. After the vet had cleaned Kitty up, we discovered that in fact she had lost an eye and some teeth. Her mouth was also a little twisted, probably, the vet thought, due to a head injury affecting the facial nerves.

'She might not be able to eat properly,' the vet warned us. 'She might not survive.'

But we were determined that Kitty be given another chance. She therefore came home with us to join Bibby and Twink. We hoped that the vet was wrong and that Kitty would regain the ability to eat solid food but she never did. She even struggled with the soft pate-type cat food we tried. Then Geoff hit upon an idea. We had an old kitchen blender that we never used. Into this we put normal cat food plus some supplements for Kitty. The ingredients were then blended into a meaty 'soup' for her. This she loved and slurped it up with relish. However, we had to feed her either in the garden (if it was warm) or in the *marquise* because as much soup ended up on the walls as did in Kitty's mouth. She also had to be laboriously cleaned after each meal to remove the soup from her whiskers and fur. Bibby and Twink sometimes helped with this; they were always keen to supplement their own meals by licking any scraps of food off Kitty's fur.

On cold days, the three of them could be found piled into their cat bed in front of the stove. Kitty was always at the bottom of the pile because Twink and Bibby used her as a hot water bottle. But she loved the attention. She adored Bibby and seemed rather in awe of Twink, a development we found rather worrying given Twink's danger-loving tendencies. To stop her jumping, Twink was still allowed onto the lane for a couple of hours a day and Kitty increasingly insisted on accompanying her. Despite her disabilities, the little cat was full of energy. However, her time outside was strictly limited and we watched her like hawks.

Beatriz often saved portions of meaty sauce to tempt Kitty but her favourite was Twink. She was astonished at our habit of picking Twink up and cuddling her, something she had never done with her own cats. Twink loved to be handled and would happily sit in your arms all day if she had the chance. Rather tentatively at first, Beatriz would pick Twink up and chatter sweet nothings at her. Twink took Beatriz' rather awkward handling in her stride and allowed herself to be manhandled. After all, she knew that Beatriz would probably be round the next day with a special treat for her 'Tweeenk.' And Beatriz usually was.

14

Now that we had some sort of income, albeit a modest one, we began to think about more improvements to the house. We had managed to save a little money for this purpose as our outgoings were so minimal. Geoff cooked from scratch and the garden was producing more food all the time. We rarely went out, partly because we were content to spend time round the house and garden but also because Geoff's dialysis sessions took up some of the week.

However, although things were busier, we tried to find time to slow down and remind ourselves of why we had moved to Porto in the first place. Sometimes we caught the bus to Gaia centre and wandered down through the little alleys to the riverfront. One evening, we found a little Moroccan restaurant that we hadn't noticed before. We were shown upstairs to a large airy dining room that, because it was so early in the evening, was gloriously empty. Beautiful wooden shutters opened onto a balcony bordered with wrought iron railings. We had the place to ourselves, so after our meal we wandered onto the balcony to admire the dusky light as the last rays of the sun glowed on the river.

The addition of fish to our diet expanded the range

of dining options open to us. When visiting Porto on holiday, we had often wandered through the backstreets of the Ribeira looking in vain for a restaurant that served interesting vegetarian food. One evening, we had been greeted by the owner of one small establishment, who was standing outside enjoying the cool evening air. Were we looking for good food and excellent wine, he asked. We were. Would we like to hear some excellent fado music while we ate? We certainly would. Before he could usher us inside, we asked if he had any vegetarian options on the menu. He froze, then quickly recovering his composure he nodded brightly. But of course, he smiled, we could have *salada mista*! As he said this, his hands swept the air in front of him in an expansive gesture that expressed the wonders of this particular dish. As we had already eaten *salada mista* in Portugal and knew that it consisted of lettuce, tomato, and grated carrot, we declined his offer and moved on.

Now, however, we had rather more options. One evening, we found a tiny fish restaurant in a steep back street by the river. We managed to get one of the three tables situated outside the restaurant with a stunning view of the river. We ate perfectly cooked sea bream and drank crisp *vinho verde* while watching the lights of the port wine lodges reflecting on the water.

But there were treasures closer to home too. If we were feeling energetic we could wander down to the river beach near our village. This was accessed through a maze of narrow cobbled alleyways and steep flights of steps that had been built into the hillside. Scattered houses perched on these ancient vertiginous lanes, their high walls hiding lush gardens and interesting outbuildings.

The old lady who washed her saucepans down at the spring lived in one of these houses, her front door opening straight onto the lane. Along the front of the house, pots of bright begonias and geraniums spilled onto the lane and a bench had been placed to catch the sun. If the weather was dry she was guaranteed to be sitting on the bench with her next door neighbour putting the world to rights.

At the bottom of the hill, the lane wound past some allotments that were fed by a fast-flowing stream and then turned into a sandy track which emerged onto the river road. This road followed the river for miles. Crossing the road you reached a beach of soft sand, which was usually deserted. It was a peaceful place to sit, watching the few little boats that bobbed on the river and gazing at the wooded slopes on the other side. From here, you could see Porto in the distance down river. But this quiet spot always seemed like a world away from the bustle of the city.

We usually walked a short distance down the river road to a small cafe that overlooked the river. Not on the way to anywhere, the place was used only by locals and was refreshingly utilitarian. The interior looked like it hadn't been decorated since the 1960s. The old glass counter was at the back of a long dimly lit room which gave onto a back room dominated by an ancient pool table. There was an outside lavatory accessed via a secluded yard filled with plants. The first time we went in there the owner looked genuinely nervous. Our own neighbourhood was now sanguine about the presence of *os Ingleses*, but the river road residents didn't know us.

Sipping our cold beer at an outside table and watching the white seeds of the poplar trees float down the road, we speculated that the owner was probably wondering how to tell us that we were way off track for the port wine lodges and therefore impossibly lost.

One day, walking past the allotments on our way home, we bumped into our builder Jorge, who tended one of the smaller allotments in his spare time. He gave us a bag of courgettes and a lift back up the hill, both of which were very welcome, and we sounded him out about the additional work we were considering on the house.

In the original round of building work, Jorge had tidied up the roof and fixed a few tiles. Now we thought we had enough money to pay for the roof to be completely replaced. We also wanted some work done on the cellar, which was rather dilapidated and fit only for the storage of garden tools. We reasoned that if the place was tiled and plastered and had electricity it would be an ideal prepping space in which to store garden produce and dried goods. Jorge promised to call us with a quote for the work.

After the debacle with installing the stove, we had decided against hiring Motta for any more work. God only knows what damage he had done to the roof anyway, sitting up there for hours hammering. We had discovered that Beatriz' faith in Motta had also been shaken after she had hired him to do some work on her own roof.

The day had been hot and she had offered Motta tea and mineral water but he had insisted on beer. She had brought him a bottle of Superbock ... and then another one. Thereafter, every twenty minutes or so, Motta had called out for more.

'Senhora, senhora! Superbock! Superbock!' Beatriz pulled her baseball cap lower over her eyes and did an excellent impression of Motta's heavy stance.

And the roof still leaked, she declared. But although Beatriz had vowed never to hire Motta again, she relented one morning after being kept awake all night by a mouse scuttling around the house. She had chased the mouse into the kitchen where it had disappeared behind the cupboards. She phoned Motta, who was confident he could catch the mouse. He came round with his hammer and pulled out all of Beatriz' kitchen cupboards. Alarmed, the mouse sprinted round the kitchen and into the sitting room, with Motta in hot pursuit. The chase lasted most of the day, only ending when the mouse disappeared into a hole in the skirting board. Beatriz was furious.

Motta reluctantly acknowledged defeat and unhelpfully declared that Beatriz needed a cat. Beatriz in fact had three cats, but they usually accompanied her to The Ledge each morning, ate the *piri piri* spaghetti she put out for the stray cats, and then spent the day on the lane stalking seagulls and torturing lizards.

If we had needed another good reason not to ask Motta to tackle any more building work, it came when, after making some improvements to his own fireplace, he managed to set his chimney on fire. We had seen clouds of dark smoke spiralling up from Motta's but had assumed he had lit one of his bonfires. But then a fire engine screamed down the lane, drawing everyone from their houses. According to Beatriz, the fire service had been distinctly unimpressed and had told Motta so in no uncertain terms. We never saw smoke from his chimney again.

Motta's growing reputation as a jinx in all matters concerning building work perhaps explained why when Novo Man needed a wall building in his garden, he didn't hire Motta. The wall was only low, about a metre in height, and was meant to border the terrace that overlooked the chicken house. The Novos' garden was clearly visible from our sitting room window and for nearly four weeks, the builders that Novo Man hired afforded us many hours of wicked amusement.

There were two of them. One was quite tall and built like a tank. The other was older and was short and wiry. He was obviously the brains behind the project. The two reminded us for all the world of Laurel and Hardy. It soon became evident that neither of them had built a wall before. They worked extremely slowly. Laurel could often be seen standing and staring at their work with a puzzled expression on his face. Whenever Laurel wasn't looking, Hardy sat down and gazed gloomily at his knees.

The stones that were to form the wall were collected from various corners of the Novos' garden, which was rather untended in places. Laurel energetically directed Hardy in the collecting of the stones and their arrangement to form a wall. We hoped it was not going to be a drystone wall, because for some reason, most of the smaller stones seemed to be going on the bottom layer of the construction.

About halfway through the project, they had obviously had second thoughts about the construction because Hardy could be seen dismantling the shaky structure and placing the stones into different piles according to size. We were relieved when construction started again, this time with the bigger stones forming the base of the wall. But then disaster struck. Hardy had spent all afternoon trying to heave a huge rectangular stone into position using a large stout metal pole as a lever. Laurel had supervised, chivvying and nagging, until the stone was almost in position at the edge of the terrace. One final heave and it would be in place. But Hardy was tired, the afternoon was hot, and the ground was uneven at the end of the terrace. His final heave-ho was badly judged and the huge stone, instead of lying neatly in position at the edge of the terrace, rolled off completely and onto the roof of the chicken shack, which promptly collapsed under the weight.

Luckily, it being summer, the chicken house was empty. Its inhabitants, who were scratching at the almost bare earth of their run, paused momentarily in their activity to watch as their shack came to rest in a pile of rubble. We couldn't help it. The expressions on the faces of Laurel and

Hardy sent us both into fits of helpless giggles.

Novo Man came out of the house and looked with astonishment at the remains of the shack. Hardy clamboured down from the terrace and hastily starting picking up bits of wood and corrugated iron and flinging them about ineffectually. To Novo Man's credit, he seemed fairly philosophical about the whole thing, and the three of them spent the next two days rebuilding the shack into the eyesore it had previously been.

We had agreed a price with Jorge for the work on the roof and early one morning he arrived with his lads in his ancient white truck. In stark contrast to Laurel and Hardy, Jorge's gang worked at a tremendous pace. They removed all the old terracotta tiles from the roof and laid a layer of a waterproofing material called *onduline*. Then they fitted new tiles and gutters. The cellar walls were lined and plastered, the floor tiled, and the whole room rewired. Both jobs were completed within days. The weather was fine so there was nothing to hinder their progress. Nothing, that is, until Twink became interested in the work.

Bibby had sensibly stayed on the patio roof well out of the builders' way. Twink, however, had other ideas. For the first two days, she sat on the patio closely observing the builders. Then, once all the old roof tiles had been removed, her curiosity got the better of her and she sneaked up to take a look. Not only was she hindering the builders, we were also worried she would get into the roof space and hurt herself. But it was difficult to stop her. Twink's sweet nature was matched by a deep streak of wilfulness and a taste for danger. In response to our entreaties for her to come down, she would shoot us a disdainful glance and then continue her quest to find a hole to stick her nose in.

Ironically, the cats ended up causing the builders more

trouble on the ground. Shortly after acquiring the kittens Geoff had built them a den on the patio out of spare bits of wood. Here Bibby, Twink, and Kitty spent the night, curled up on a pile of old blankets. We went onto the patio one afternoon to find one of the builders scratching himself frantically. When he saw us, he pointed at Twink, who was sitting on the jacket he had left on the bench. 'Pulgas!' he yelled.

We assured him that our cats certainly did not have fleas.

'Pulgas,' he insisted.

'Não, não,' we assured him.

Jorge and one of the other lads came down off the roof to find out what was happening. By this time, their colleague was hopping up and down on the patio scratching and shouting. At one point, he stopped and pulled down his work trousers to show us the supposed fleabites on his legs. Jorge and his mate guffawed and Geoff and I tried to hide our smiles.

Jorge said something in a low voice to us, which we didn't catch, and told the lad in no uncertain terms to pull his trousers up and get back to work. We knew the cats were clean as they were all checked regularly. Besides, none of the rest of us had seen any fleas. From this, and from Jorge's attitude, we could only conclude that the unfortunate scratcher was a little neurotic. We wondered whether the trait was common in builders, perhaps a result of too much sun (readers of our previous book *Escape to the Hills* will surely be drawing comparisons here between Scratcher and poor Peter, who worked on our house in Liverpool).

The next day, Scratcher was calmer but rather sullen. He cheered up the following day, by which time he had stopped scratching. On the day the work was finished and the builders took their leave, Scratcher presented us with a gift ... a bottle of flea repellent! It was powerful stuff, he said, he had apparently doused himself daily in the stuff and Look! No more fleas!

We smiled and thought it best to say nothing. At least he seemed happier now. However, we noticed that he gave Twink rather a dark look before he left.

We hoped that the new roof would mean an end to the leaks we occasionally experienced during heavy rain. Portuguese houses are not built to cope with rain. Normally the roof tiles are simply laid on the rafters, which means that water can easily find its way through. Unlike in the UK, windows and doors have no drip ledges to guide the rain away.

Our beautiful full-length doors in the bedroom, for instance, sat straight onto a stone step which continued into the room to meet the floorboards. Across this step, a runnel had been carefully carved. When it rained heavily, the water seeped under the door and was caught in the runnel where it was channelled back outside through a narrow hole carved into the stone for this purpose. The stone window sills throughout the house had a similar design. Attractive and ingenious though this solution was, we often wondered why the original builders had not simply constructed the doors and windows to keep out the rain in the first place.

Evidence of a similar lack of common sense about rainfall can be seen in the design of Portuguese gutters. The new gutters that Jorge fitted were just like the old ones in one important characteristic: they were completely level. This meant that any water that was caught stayed in the gutter and didn't run out into the water butts we had carefully installed. The sole point of a gutter is to take runoff water away. This was the one thing our nice new gutters didn't do. In fact so much water comes off the kitchen roof that its gutter fills up in seconds and spills the water all down the *marquise* wall.

We have concluded that the cause of this strange neglect reflects a tendency for denial of anything to do with rain. Portugal typically enjoys a lot of warm and dry weather, so cool and wet conditions are not treated with the kind of sanguine acceptance of the inevitable that is widespread in the UK. If an unusual cold or wet snap occurred in summer, we often saw our neighbours walking down the lane, heads bent stubbornly against the cold and wet but not a jacket or cardigan in sight. It is as if protecting yourself and your house against the elements is an admission that the weather will let you down. The possession of a coat or a functioning set of gutters would surely stop the sun coming out again!

As I write this, there are rumours that the EU is planning to require homeowners to comply with new regulations that make homes more environmentally friendly and energy efficient. Owners that do not, for instance, install insulation and make other improvements by 2030 will be forced to move out of their homes. We await these developments with interest, because from what we have seen of Portuguese houses, the new directive will involve practically the whole population being forced onto the streets!

Inclement conditions are routinely blamed on São Pedro, the patron saint of weather. Beatriz was particularly vociferous in this respect. Her own house was large and rarely heated so she was always grumpy during periods of bad weather. She would grumble about how São Pedro needed to pull his socks up, so to speak, and do something about the cold, the wind, or the torrential rain. Once, during a sudden hailstorm, I even saw her shake a small fist at the sky.

Although we were now living in a warmer climate, we

seemed to be battling with the same domestic problems we had faced at our cottage in North Wales. We both preferred older houses; they have more soul and character. They also tend to have more damp and other sorts of problems. But the nice thing about an old house is that it is more organic, more in tune with its environment. The little colonies of mildew on the inside of the north-facing walls wax and wane according to the season. The old wooden doors and window frames swell and contract with the heat and the cold and damp, and the locks seize up and then loosen again. Even the water in the boiler and the cistern flow differently in summer compared to winter. In cold weather, the ant colonies that live in the cracks in the concrete garden paths find their way through cracks in the sitting room wall to take up residence behind the sideboard. In summer, the sparrows return to the sitting room gutter to build their nests and raise their noisy broods, scolding us shrilly whenever we go into that part of the garden.

We consider our house to be like our lives: a work in progress. The house will never be free of spiders, dust, or the odd patch of mildew. We will never have air conditioning, underfloor heating, or a bespoke designer kitchen. But in its quirky, comfortable, characterful way, the house feeds our imagination, and in the words of the philosopher Gaston Bachelard, has taught us to 'abide within ourselves' in this unfamiliar country we are still learning to call home.

15

Our position on the lane meant that we had an excellent vantage point from which to observe the various activities and daily rhythms of our little neighbourhood. We sometimes imagined our house as the centre of an orrery, those old clockwork models of the solar system that represent the positions and movement of the planets around the sun. Over the course of the day, we watched the same characters pass our house, busy in their daily routines.

We two had also fallen into a pleasing pattern of work and leisure. We liked to start the day slowly, lingering over toasted bread rolls and a large *café meia de leite*, a comforting mix of espresso and hot milk. The double aspect windows in the sitting room meant that from our perch on the sofa, the centre of the orrery, we could watch the comings and goings on the lane. We knew everyone's usual routines and they knew ours. There was something reassuring about that.

In fact, any change in our usual habits would often prompt concern. One of the elderly ladies who lived in the next lane passed our house every day on her way to the shops. It was a mystery to us why Senhora Angelina shopped every day, as she lived alone. But rain or shine, she would toil up the hill every day except for Sundays, returning completely laden down with heavy bags, and usually a mop bucket, a new broom, or some other household implement. Judging by her purchases, she probably possessed the cleanest house in Portugal.

If we happened to be in the garden, we waved to her and exchanged greetings. One July, I had been ill with a bad summer cold and so hadn't been out much. When I was recovered, I saw her on the lane. She carefully put down her shopping bags and stopped to talk. She hadn't seen me for a while, she said, and she had been worried. Was I alright?

We, in turn, would become concerned if any of the elements that made up the orrery were missing or out of place. The machinery of the orrery was already in motion before we rose. At about four o'clock in the morning, a small motorcycle would pass the house carrying the local baker to work. Half-awoken from dreams, we would think *Baker Biker* before drifting off again. At sevenish, The Man with the Dog could be heard, taking Fofo for his morning constitutional. Opening the shutters, we might glimpse Alta Man, already pottering round his garden. Shortly afterwards, we would hear the postman going by on his scooter. Like a small tornado, he sped up and down the narrow lanes. The high walls bordering the lanes would magnify and distort the sound of his engine, so that for a moment, we would stop what we were doing, puzzled at the sound, before realizing it was the postie rather than some weird atmospheric compression event.

Sipping our breakfast coffee on the sofa, we would soon see the mid-morning cafe run: Beatriz' husband António would hurry past, trying to keep up with a neighbour we called Speedy Man. This character could frequently be seen on the lane as he visited the cafe about four times a day. He always passed a few comments in greeting to us as he walked past but, as he never slowed down, his words were usually snatched away on the breeze and therefore impossible to catch for us novice Portuguese speakers.

The neighbourhood women had their own distinct daily habits. At around mid-morning, the fish seller, who drove like a woman possessed, would race up in her small silver van. Ten minutes later, the bread van would arrive. But a good forty minutes before their arrival, Maria, Lena, and Nova Lady would be waiting on the lane. They would lean comfortably on Not Manuel's wall and gossip, pausing only to call down advice to Not Manuel, who would now be back from the cafe and gently hoeing his vegetable patch, a cigarette dangling from his lips.

When we started eating fish again, we sometimes joined the little queue at the fish van to buy fresh sardines or hake. In the early days, before Geoff started baking bread, we also bought rolls, baguettes, and cakes from the bread van, which stopped directly outside our gate before continuing to the corner where Maria and the other ladies waited. Hearing the van's horn, I would hurriedly throw on a cardigan and shoes, because the bread man didn't hang around. The only other customers at 'our' stop were The Man with the Dog and a character we called the Shy Man, who lived somewhere up the hill. The Shy Man was friendly but very reserved and hardly said a word to anyone. Even though he had only come out to buy bread, he was always impeccably dressed. Under his pale tailored suit he wore a waistcoat and you could sometimes glimpse a watch chain hanging from his waistcoat pocket. His shoes were highly polished and his silver hair was always combed and arranged precisely.

With the bread and fish sellers gone and lunchtime approaching, there was a lull on the lane, unless Malcolm was on the road. If he was repairing a motorcycle, he would test drive it up and down the lane, waving cheerily to passing pedestrians. Malcolm's son, Ricardo, was less considerate. He rode a motorcycle with a souped-up engine (probably tuned by Malcolm to sound like an approaching hurricane) and took obvious pleasure in razzing down the lane as fast and as loudly as he could. If he came round the corner unexpectedly it was wise to flatten yourself against the wall while he sped past. It was a mystery to everyone who exactly Ricardo was trying to impress, as everyone he roared past would shake their heads and roll their eyes at the noise. Beatriz always looked like she would have pushed him off his bike if she could.

In Portugal, each neighbourhood has a communal set of refuse bins rather than individual bins. These bins are emptied every day. Our bins were on the corner of the lane not far from The Ledge. Taking out the rubbish therefore involved a longer or shorter daily walk, depending on how far your house was from the bins. At about six in the morning, the bin wagon crawled slowly down the lane past the sleeping houses. Because it was electric, its progress was almost silent. Once parked by the bins, however, the bin men then threw the assorted *lixo* into the wagon with such gusto that the whole neighbourhood was rudely awoken to bangs, thumps, and crashes.

On fine afternoons, Senhora Angelina and her friend could usually be seen in their gardening hats and overalls carrying bags and buckets stuffed with garden waste to the bin. I have already explained the suspicion with which the practice of composting is regarded. Accordingly, in the summer months, the bins overflowed with vine prunings, leaves, and weeds as our neighbours got their gardens in order.

We observed that some people made a weekly rather

than a daily pilgrimage to the bins. We knew one couple who lived near Alta Man and who drove an ancient Ford Cortina. They were very chatty and if we saw their car on the lane they would always stop and wind down the window to talk. They both looked about seventy years old. Senhor Cortina wore the smart trousers and jacket popular with older Portuguese men. Senhora Cortina, in contrast, wore what she had no doubt worn in the 1970s: flared jeans, gaudy printed blouses with enormous collars, smocks, and embroidered waistcoats.

Every Sunday, the Cortinas would drive down the lane painfully slowly and park at the bins. They would unload from the car a week's work of *lixo*, which always contained a hefty amount of green waste and two buckets full of food scraps. It was Senhora Cortina who did the driving and this was frequently a source of contention between them. It is an understatement to say that the lady did not have a facility for driving; even though she drove at a snail's pace, the car was pockmarked with dents and covered with scratches. Senhor Cortina could often be seen climbing out of the passenger seat to direct her at difficult points of the lane. When she didn't follow his directions, he would get exasperated, at which point she would wind down the window and shout at him.

One Sunday we were on the patio when we saw their car heading down the lane. They slowed to wave at Beatriz, who was feeding the cats at The Ledge. Unfortunately, this encounter distracted Senhora Cortina, and the car suddenly started to roll downhill towards Not Manuel's garden. Only a small ledge separated the road from the garden, which dropped steeply below the level of the road. Beatriz started frantically waving her arms in alarm, cats scattering around her. Just as the car was about to reach the edge of the road, Senhora Cortina slammed on the brakes.

Beatriz crossed herself and cast her eyes heavenwards. Senhor and Senhora Cortina got out of the car and started to squabble. Beatriz went over to adjudicate.

Eventually, the Cortinas got back in the car and parked it at the bins to offload their rubbish. This done, Senhora Cortina began to execute her usual ten-point turn prior to making the return journey. This was a tricky task at the best of times, but that day she was still arguing heatedly with Senhor Cortina. After one manoeuvre, there was a loud crunch as she backed the car into a wall.

After this unfortunate incident, we never saw the car again. However, the Cortinas were nothing if not resourceful and they soon had a replacement vehicle: a homemade handcart. This was piled so high with *lixo* that it took two of them to push it. We could hear them coming down the hill because the wheels badly squeaked. One day, they laboured down the lane with a particularly full cart, only to find that the bin men had briefly taken the bins away to be cleaned. The Cortinas stared at the empty space in disbelief. They walked up and down the lane a little way, as if the bins might have migrated on their own to another spot overnight. Finally, they gave up and pushed their loaded cart back up the hill.

Superimposed upon the daily and weekly rhythms of our neighbours were the more infrequent cycles of visitors to the neighbourhood. When we went up to Mrs Costa's, we often saw a silver-haired couple who lived near the shop and who always stopped for a brief chat. They were about the same age as the Cortinas, and were well-known in the area as enthusiastic walkers. They spent most of the day strolling round the lanes; sometimes they walked along our lane on their way down to the river. I don't know how they did it, but they walked for miles.

Mrs Costa told us one day that she was on a car journey

with her nephew and she saw the couple out walking in the next parish, several miles from where they lived. The curious thing was, they never seemed to be dressed for long treks. He would wear his usual trousers, jacket, and loafers, and she would be dressed tidily in a skirt, a little blouse, and smart court shoes. Hardly the attire for hiking.

The rhythms of the orrery became somewhat less predictable in festival season. At the midsummer festival of São João, our little lane became busy with the visits of various friends and relatives to our neighbours' homes. We had been introduced to the São João festival by chance one afternoon. We had gone to our favourite cafe in Batalha for lunch. Emerging from the cafe into the sunlight of the square we suddenly found ourselves surrounded by people. Praça de Batalha was full of stalls selling cakes, crafts, and little terracotta pots containing basil plants. There was a party atmosphere to the crowd; people were bopping each other on the head with squeaky plastic hammers and waving garlic flowers.

Beatriz told us later that these were traditional activities linked with the feast of São João. On the night of the festival, the streets, cafes, and bars of Porto are full. The most dedicated partygoers finish the evening by walking downriver to the Foz do Douro district, where they sit on the beach to watch the sun rise.

But as well as celebrating São João, every parish and community in Porto holds its own smaller religious and social festivals. Throughout the year there are regular callers at our gate, collecting for these little *festas*, which are funded by the community. Our doorbell also rings to the sound of other, less frequent callers selling various goods, from socks to saucepans. I think the pedlars like our neighbourhood as it is leafy and calm and affords a pleasant view of the river.

One warm day, there was a ring at the bell. Opening the gate, I found a short rotund man standing there with a wheelbarrow. He was wearing ancient flip-flops and a tattered straw hat.

He greeted me with a 'Boa tarde' followed by 'Olhe!'

We had been curious about this latter expression. 'Ohle' literally means 'see.' We had noticed that the word was often used when you wanted to draw someone's attention to something; kind of like a 'Look here' or 'See here'.

What Senhor Ohle wanted to draw my attention to was his wheelbarrow, which was full of large sacks of potatoes.

'Ohle,' he repeated, and pointed at the potatoes. He told me that he had picked them just yesterday. He worked for an old lady who owned a large *quinta* near the river and had an enormous garden in which she grew vegetables. But how was she to sell these marvellous vegetables? This was where Senhor Ohle came in. Out of the goodness of his heart he was helping her to get rid of her surplus produce and *Graças a Deus*, she had only a few sacks of potatoes left. Would we help the old lady and buy a sack at the ridiculously low price he was offering?

On hearing this ridiculously low price, Geoff, who had come out to see who was at the gate, muttered to me, 'These are more expensive than supermarket prices!'

However, the potatoes were of excellent quality and we always liked to buy in bulk. Senhor Ohle's story was a little far-fetched, but we preferred to see money go to local growers rather than straight to the big supermarkets. We therefore bought a sack of potatoes from Ohle, who subsequently wandered off to bother our neighbours. We suspected he had no luck for he was last seen at the bottom of the hill, contemplating the steep climb back up the lane. With flip-flops and a heavy wheelbarrow, we didn't fancy his chances.

An important hub of activity in the neighbourhood was the old *lavadouro*. While most people went down there to wash clothes or collect water from the spring, others used it for different purposes. The little lady of course washed her saucepans in the spring and Matilde sometimes gutted fish down there, rinsing them in the flowing spring water. We could always tell when she had been down there because there would be a couple of skinny cats sniffing about and the lichen that coated the stones would be studded with shiny scales that glinted in the sunlight.

An elderly lady who lived in a tiny cottage near Mrs Costa's shop sometimes came down to the spring to wash her hair. She had very long hair that was a beautiful shade of silver. She told me one day that she refused to use mains water on her hair because it was too harsh. Instead, once a week she made the journey down to the spring. In her colourful long skirts and shawls, she looked like a visitor from the long-distant past.

In very warm weather the *lavadouro* was irresistible to the local children. If there was no-one washing down there they would strip off and leap in to splash about in the cool water. Occasionally, one or two of the local dogs would do the same. But woe betide kids and dogs if they got caught by Matilde or one of her cronies!

Just as the *lavadouro* was a centre of camaraderie for the local women, it was sometimes used as an impromptu meeting place for the men, as it was a pleasant sheltered place to sit. One Christmas Eve, we went down to collect spring water and found two men down there, sitting and chatting near the spring, an old dog at their feet. They had come to collect water and were now taking the time to have a smoke and a festive bottle of beer or two. They greeted us merrily and wished us a *Feliz Natal*. We chatted briefly but declined their offer of beer, and after exchanging New

Year greetings made our escape through a haze of cigarette smoke.

The neighbourhood animals had their own rhythms. Each morning and afternoon, the cats on The Ledge waited for Beatriz to appear with scraps. Because we were so near the river, the seagulls quickly discovered this interesting new source of food and learnt when Beatriz was due. The cats in their turn considered the seagulls a new and interesting, though unattainable, source of food. The more optimistic street cats, like Laranja, spent hours fruitlessly stalking any seagulls that landed on The Ledge.

At midday, the street cats would disappear for a snooze and the seagulls would clean The Ledge of anything the cats had turned their noses up at. The practice of feeding meal scraps to the dogs and cockerels meant that at lunchtimes, the neighbourhood would ring to the sound of barking dogs and calling cockerels vying for the attention of their owners. About twice a week, just after lunch, Matilde's dog Senhor Mário would break out of his enclosure and sprint down the road joyfully, followed shortly by Matilde herself, sweating and flustered. She refused to upset him by tying him up in the garden, and Mário took advantage of this by breaking out as often as he could.

On summer afternoons, we loved watching the swallows swoop through the little valley, catching insects on the wing. We celebrated their arrival in spring and mourned their departure at the end of summer. The *andorinha*, the swallow, is a popular mascot in Portugal, representing as it does faithfulness, love, and home. The eaves of Motta's old house were a popular nesting site for the swallows and during nesting season, Nova Lady's cats would climb onto Motta's roof, lie on the edge, and dangle their paws down to the eaves. The swallows would swoop around their nests, screaming in protest at the invasion.

On hot clear days we would sometimes spot a couple of buzzards circling way up high, riding the hot thermals. Their mewing was a welcome sound as it reminded us of our mountain home in North Wales. On winter nights, another echo back to our previous home could be heard in the hooting and screeching of the owls in the big oak tree in Alta Man's garden. Although we often heard the owls, they were difficult to spot. The bats, however, were easy to observe if you went and stood in the garden or on the lane at dusk. Like the swallows, the bats worked the network of little streams that flowed across the hill and fed the spring. If you stood for a minute or two and let yourself become accustomed to the gloom, you could soon spot the little shapes, darting and cornering at impossible speeds, little spirits of the shadows.

A less welcome fixture of the neighbourhood were the cars. Although our semi-rural location was much quieter than where we had lived in Liverpool, it wasn't exactly traffic-free. Although there weren't many houses on our lane, there were plenty of cars. One reason for this is the fact that multigenerational living is quite common in Portugal (and is becoming more common in other countries). Many of the houses on our lane contained two or even three generations of families.

Many of the larger older dwellings in Portugal are so-called 'island houses'. These consist of several small houses, or sections of the same house, built around a courtyard. We had viewed one of these island houses in Porto when we were house-hunting. Our own house, although now one dwelling, had originally housed three generations of the same family. The house had been gradually extended and added on to as the family had grown, and each new part of the house had its own house number. The plethora of these houses, which are often surrounded by high walls, may reflect the hard times experienced under Salazar's authoritarian regime.

Modern multigenerational living can generate a strong sense of family and community, as the same families may remain in an area for generations. However, one downside of this is a lack of personal space. Like many younger people nowadays, few of the young adults in our neighbourhood could afford to pay rent or take out a mortgage. The increasing popularity of living in vans or tiny homes is testament to the current widening gap between wages and housing costs.

Many of our neighbours had young adult children still living with them. We speculated that owning a car was particularly important to people living with parents and/or grandparents. Unable to afford a house or apartment of their own, their cars at least afforded a little private space.

The traffic noise on the lane was made worse by the fact that most of our neighbours drove cars that were rather old and rickety. Susana's son Rui drove an ancient Mercedes that belched smoke and struggled on the hills. Motta's car looked and sounded like a small scrap yard. But these vehicles seemed in fantastic condition compared to the ones we sometimes heard driving down the lane at night. On some nights, we heard the most appalling clanks and rattles, and could only guess at the state of the vehicles that they issued from. We imagined sometimes a whole section of the population driving round after dark in cars that were unroadworthy and gloriously free of road tax or insurance.

The persistence of older traditions and the tendency (or necessity) of keeping older vehicles and equipment going as long as possible meant that we sometimes felt out of time. About once a month, what looked like a black 1940s Chevrolet crawled down the lane, driven by an equally old gentleman who wore driving gloves and a tweed cap.

We always scrambled to see him as he passed, but have never managed to get close enough to satisfy our curiosity about both car and driver. We sometimes wonder if anyone else sees him, or whether it is just some strange time slip specific to ourselves.

One day, we heard the rumbling of a large engine on the lane and looked up to see an elderly man trundling by perched on an antiquated rotavator. We couldn't help laughing out loud, for we had seen a machine just like it the previous evening watching an old episode of the 1970s British television sitcom *The Good Life*. The sitcom tells the story of Tom and Barbara, a couple who decide to leave the rat race to pursue their dream of self-sufficiency by growing vegetables and raising animals in their garden in the suburbs. In the episode we had watched, Tom is seen riding down the tidy suburban road on practically the same rotavator, which was antiquated even in the 1970s!

It was true that our little neighbourhood could be noisy and a little raucous at times. The shouts and singing from the *lavadouro*, the cacophony of the cockerels, cats, dogs, and children, the visits of the bread seller, fish seller, scrap merchant, and farm vehicles all broke the peaceful silence of the ancient lanes and the green hillside. But they breathed life into the place, they made it a living community rather than a gentrified relic of the past.

Near where we lived in Snowdonia, there was a little village that we often drove through on our way to Llangollen. The village was very pretty; chocolate box houses lay peacefully along a lane bordered by lush hedgerows. A little stream ran through the village, which was surrounded by picture postcard views of the hills. But the place was lifeless. It was inhabited by retired people and commuters. There were no children climbing the trees, no hub around which the local people gathered, no chickens clucking in the too-tidy gardens. If someone had set up an impromptu barbecue on the street corner, the police would probably have been summoned.

Remnants of the past were there: an abandoned corner shop, a boarded-up village well. But now nobody drew the sweet spring water or discussed the price of fresh fish. The surrounding farmland was dotted with sheep; there were no human figures to be seen in the fields, working the land. There was no annual harvest and no local midsummer festivals. The villagers bought their eggs and vegetables from the supermarket in Llandudno. If you sat drinking your breakfast coffee by the window in one of the gentrified cottages, you would see no daily orrery, no bustle, no village life.

Of course, the village would have been different a hundred years ago. As in our Portuguese neighbourhood, people would have grown food in their gardens, kept a few animals. There would have been smaller farms, more cottage industries, more local bartering. No doubt these aspects of life will slowly disappear in Portugal too, as the traditional rhythms of community life die out and global forces displace local traditions. Our enjoyment of our lively little neighbourhood was therefore tinged by the bittersweet flavour of *saudade*, by the knowledge that we were observing a way of life that would probably soon be lost.

16

After ten years of living in the wilderness in Wales, spending half our time being academics in the city and half living like peasants in our primitive cottage, we wanted more than anything a change of pace.

Although initially seduced by the prospect of buying a cheap ruin with acres of land in the Portuguese countryside, we had opted to stay closer to the city and settle for something smaller. We knew that our *quintinha* would never produce all the food we needed, but, we reasoned, it didn't have to. Fresh, seasonal, local produce was widely available in Portugal and it was cheap. We had baked all our own bread in the UK; here, delicious fresh bread could be bought from the bread van right outside our own front door.

We pictured ourselves living a more cosmopolitan, less frenetic life than we had led in the UK. We would have just a small garden in which we would grow a few choice plants. Like the Portuguese themselves, we would eat out more and go to the beach. We would focus on our writing rather than on tending the land. We would travel a little.

Life, of course, has its own agenda, and perhaps it is good that we usually get what we need rather than what we think we want. A combination of lack of money and Geoff's illness had demanded from us flexibility and hard decision-making. Our oft-imagined dream of pottering around Porto in the Iberian sunshine with not a care in the world began to seem a tad naive.

Instead, we spent most of our time around the house and garden. Apart from trips to the dialysis clinic and Mrs Costa's *mini-mercado*, we rarely went out. I gradually picked up more work copyediting and Geoff wrote and worked in the garden, depending on his energy levels.

In a strange way, this period probably helped us to put down roots, not just in our adopted community but in relation to our home and little plot of land, which suddenly became much more important to us. We had initially visualized our little place in Porto as just a base from which to explore, a point from which to expand and have further adventures. We slowly realized that in fact we needed the opposite; a chance to slow down, to rest, to retreat. Forced to turn inward, we gradually experienced a greater sense of connectedness to our new home.

And working in the garden provided a respite for Geoff from the stress of dialysis. There, he could lose himself in his plants and calm his mind. Sowing, planting, digging, and watering helped his physical and psychological fitness. But the garden didn't just provide therapy. We had always tried to grow as much of our own food as possible but now we were on a limited income it was even more important.

Geoff reasoned that he may not be able to easily go out to work, but he could develop our little plot to produce as much fresh fruit and vegetables as possible. In the UK, working full-time meant that the gardening had to be squeezed into pockets of time at the weekends or in the evenings. But now, what we lacked in income, we made up for in time.

In modern society, we are taught that striving for the highest possible income is a good thing. But in today's global recession, finding a well-paid job or being able to afford the training to make oneself eligible for better paid work is increasingly difficult. Many of us, whether we like it or not, are now part of the 'gig economy', with its attendant lack of benefits such as sick pay and paid holidays. One solution often offered is the pursuit of 'side hustles'; fitting in extra jobs to boost one's income and hopefully amass enough money to give up work. But taking on more work if you are struggling with health issues or are caring for children or sick relatives is easier said than done.

There is an easier option that often receives relatively less attention. Rather than striving to increase your earnings, try to reduce your outgoings. It slowly started to dawn on us that this side of the equation was more important. In the UK, a lot of our income disappeared because we both went out to work. Travel of course was a major expense, but so was buying in food and goods that we couldn't produce ourselves because we didn't have the time (because we went out to work!). It was a catch 22 situation. But now we were finally in the position to develop our own modest cottage economy.

In 2018, after being on dialysis for five years, Geoff finally received a kidney transplant. It had been a long wait. Following the surgery, he was in hospital only a week. However, the recovery process was lengthy. He had to slowly regain his strength and for the first few months after the transplant, he had to attend for monitoring at the hospital two or three times a week.

But the release from three dialysis sessions a week meant a whole new lease of life. Once he had made the initial recovery from the surgery, Geoff threw himself into growing food, cooking, and prepping. We quickly settled into a division of labour that suited our individual skills and proclivities. Geoff was by far the better cook and he was more experienced in gardening than I was. He was also stronger than me so it made sense for him to do the heavier garden work and house maintenance. I was pernickety by nature (which suited editing work!) and had more patience with office work and tight deadlines. We therefore diversified our efforts. While my job was to bring some money into the household, Geoff's job was to stop it going out.

The harsh mountain weather had ensured that growing food in our garden in Snowdonia had been challenging to say the least. In Portugal, we looked forward to the luxury of being able to grow the types of food we could only dream of in Wales: peppers, aubergines, outdoor tomatoes, maybe even peaches and kiwis!

The longer growing season certainly upped our production. Geoff sowed, planted, repotted, and then repeated the whole process throughout each growing season, trying to produce as much food as possible from our modest plot. In high summer, the garden was like an urban jungle. French beans climbed up every vertical surface, fat ripe tomatoes spilled over the paths, and huge orange squash hung from their wire framework. The longed-for peppers and aubergines ripened slowly in the sun and salad leaves grew lushly under the canopy of the grapevines.

We had sweet little ruby red beetroot, succulent spring onions (hard to find in the shops), and delicious new potatoes. Strawberries edged the borders of the garden beds and raspberries clustered in the shade. Our small lime tree produced an abundance of fruit each year and we enjoyed figs and plums in season. Geoff planted garlic and artichokes and grew kiwi fruit up the patio walls.

Beatriz disapproved of our garden design. In her own

garden, the potatoes and cabbages were not allowed to cohabit with the roses and agapanthus; Beatriz' plants had to do as they were told and keep to their designated spaces. She didn't like the way that Geoff interplanted flowers and vegetables or with the way the rhubarb grew cheek by jowl with the roses. She fretted at the way the tendrils of the squash and cucumber plants tangled lovingly around the grapevine, and she told us that some of the plants we were growing were just *ervas*, weeds.

If she called round when Geoff was in the garden she would stand and watch him gardening with a critical eye.

'Ervas!' she would say, gesturing at him to pull out various plants she didn't like the look of.

She had a particular hatred of purslane. This pretty fleshy-leaved plant grew profusely in the area, and particularly favoured Beatriz' garden. We liked the purslane, we told her. It was nice in salads. Geoff ate a leaf to demonstrate and then held one out to Beatriz who shook her head vigorously. Her son, who lived in France, ate it, she said. Everyone in France did. She screwed up her face and glared at the plant suspiciously.

Beatriz was similarly doubtful about the concept of edible flowers. In the balmy Portuguese climate the nasturtiums we planted grew all year round, and their leaves and flowers were very tasty. She flatly refused to taste a nasturtium flower and giggled when we told her we used both flowers and leaves in salads. However, she admired the scented roses, jasmine, and freesias we planted, and we gave her cuttings in exchange for the houseplant cuttings she often brought us.

Some of our favourite garden flowers were those produced by the vegetable plants. We looked forward every year to seeing the delicate white rocket flowers with their little streaks of gold, and the cool blue flowers of the endive. We interplanted African marigolds and spent the summer admiring their orange and gold rosettes dotted through the beds like swatches of rich Tudor fabric.

Our dense jumble of foliage and flowers attracted the birds and insects. Enormous furry bees and Red Admirals, Cabbage Whites, and other butterflies flittered through the garden beds on sunny days, working the flowers. As well as the sparrows, the blue tits, great tits, and occasional coal tits were regular visitors and there was always a robin or two around in the winter.

But there were other less familiar visitors that we'd never seen in our Welsh garden. In spring and summer the plum and apples trees were full of the melodic song of tiny warblers that moved so fast it was impossible to observe them closely. And everywhere, on the warm flat surfaces of the patio walls and the sheltered stone edges of the garden beds, were lizards, like little grey-green statues. The garden paths had to be navigated with care to avoid disturbing them as they basked in the sun. If you hurried through the garden, the leaves and undergrowth would rustle frantically as the lizards beat a hasty retreat.

We encouraged the birds and lizards as they helped to control pests like greenfly. The birds also sometimes added to our plant stocks by dropping seeds; one year, we discovered a bay tree and a flowering climbing plant (which has very pretty yellow flowers though we have no idea what it is) that we had definitely not planted ourselves.

Other animals were less helpful. On our hillside in Wales, we sometimes encountered water voles, small glossy creatures, darting along the edges of the water meadow, but they never ventured into the garden. Here, the voles like to dig elaborate networks of tunnels under the garden beds and eat the roots of our plants and trees. To thwart them, Geoff has moved some of the smaller apple trees and other plants into huge buckets and pots to protect them.

Our major garden nemesis in our Welsh plot consisted of slugs and snails, who munched their way through whole beds of lettuce, pak choi, and other tasty edibles. We had looked forward to gardening in a warmer, dryer climate that would surely be devoid of such pests. But it was not to be. Although the weather is certainly gentler here, we can sometimes have short periods of torrential rain that wear away the concrete paths and bring out a rash of mollusc predators. The rain will suddenly give way to long periods of hot dry weather, which have Geoff running around with watering cans trying to keep everything hydrated.

Despite the vagaries of the local weather and destructive fauna, the productivity of the garden steadily increased as Geoff devised schemes to outwit the pests and deal with the periodic drought conditions. Shopping at a local builders merchants one day, we chanced upon some enormous plastic troughs which were perfect for growing root crops like carrots and parsnips. Not only does this method protect the plants from the voles, the troughs hold water and stop the crops drying out too much. We suspected that Beatriz was horrified to see us cover the soil with black plastic containers but we didn't care; the flavoursome carrots and sweet parsnips we enjoy are worth it.

We also discovered that some varieties fare better against the pests than others. While the slugs adore the loose-leafed green lettuces, they aren't as keen on the slightly bristly leaves of red mustard or the attractively curly leaves of the endive. And they largely ignore the nasturtiums. Yet all of these plants make particularly tasty salads and we actually prefer them to some of the lettuce varieties. Geoff quickly discovered that it was easier to specialize in these hardier plants than to spend time and energy battling over those the slugs were hell-bent on eating.

Container growing also makes it easier to harvest a particular crop without disturbing the surrounding soil. This is essential when growing in a smaller space. Geoff's gardening philosophy follows the 'square inch' gardening approach; plants are packed into every bit of space possible and when one crop is harvested, another is planted in its place.

In the early years we often found ourselves hankering after a little more land. We fantasized about a larger plot that would allow us to plant up an orchard, have large beds of potatoes, maybe a polytunnel or two. But land is expensive near the city; to obtain a larger garden we would have to move into the countryside. And as we found when we lived in Wales, rural living brings its own costs. For one thing, it would mean we would have to buy a car, the expense of which would no doubt wipe out the savings gained from growing more food and maybe even keeping chickens.

We have also come to realize that we don't really want to be smallholders. Geoff worked on a farm as a teenager and has no particular wish to repeat the experience in middle age! Instead he gardens thoughtfully, with a mind to growing the foods we eat the most, and those that are less affordable in the shops. There are only two of us; we don't actually need acres of potatoes or twenty orange trees; we wouldn't eat that amount of produce and Geoff wouldn't have the time to process it. Besides, potatoes are cheap to buy at Mrs Costa's and we often receive bags of oranges from our neighbours (who cannot eat all their produce either!).

Instead, the garden provides us with the foods we eat the most and those that cost more in the shops, such as fresh new potatoes and asparagus. We have fresh pickings of organic herbs and salad leaves all year round, as well as fruit and vegetables that are harder to find in the shops, such as fresh raspberries, interesting radish varieties, and parsnips. Geoff has also experimented with growing more specialist plants, such as wasabi, watercress, and avocado. We planted root cuttings of horseradish, ginger, and turmeric and were surprised to find that these grow quite easily and flourish if they are protected over winter.

A big change in our diet has been learning to eat more seasonally. On one of our first trips to Porto, when we were still living in the UK, we went to a small cafe for lunch. Most of the delicious-looking sandwiches on offer contained meat or fish, and the woman behind the counter, seeing our hesitancy, offered to make up a sandwich with our preferred ingredients. Perhaps we would like egg or cheese? But when we asked for cheese and tomato, she looked puzzled and shook her head firmly. *Tomate*? Not possible, she said. It was March! Too early for tomatoes. Now, if we had come in June, well, then she could have offered us as much tomato as we could eat.

Of course, it is little use growing lots of produce unless you can process and preserve it. Growing food, cooking it, and preserving it in various ways is now Geoff's full-time job for most of the year. He is passionate about trying to produce as much of the food we eat at home rather than buying it in. As a consequence, our diet is better than it has ever been and even though food prices are increasing all the time, we spend less on food than we did twelve years ago. We buy only the basic ingredients that we cannot grow, such as flour, milk, eggs, pasta, and coffee (though two years ago, in a moment of optimism, we did briefly consider trying to buy a few coffee plants!).

When we can, we buy staples such as flour and porridge oats in bulk to cut costs. Nowadays we no longer visit the bread van when it comes hurtling down the lane. Instead, every fortnight, Geoff spends a day making two weeks worth of sturdy bread rolls, which we store in the freezer and use for breakfasts and lunches. He also makes any other kinds of bread or flour-based foods we need, such as fresh pitta or naan breads, tortillas, pancakes, and crackers. These are quick and easy to make and save us a substantial amount of money.

But producing our own food goes beyond issues of economy. Geoff's work in the garden and kitchen ensures that we experience a good quality of life, which is one of the reasons we moved to Portugal in the first place. Eating well is perhaps the single biggest thing anyone can do to improve their health, and home-cooked food made from fresh home-grown ingredients and prepared with love and attention is full of both vitality and taste. Working from home, we are able do as the Portuguese do, and devote more attention to mealtimes. We relish lingering over meals and having time for dessert or a mid-morning snack, rather than having to race off to the office again.

Being released from dialysis sessions meant that we were able to revert to a more satisfying meal schedule. Instead of having a large lunch followed by a snack in the evening when Geoff returned from the clinic, we switched to a modest lunch and something more substantial in the evening. Our training in Chinese medicine had impressed on us the importance of eating the right amount of food at the right time of day. Instead of skipping breakfast we have the traditional coffee and rolls, preceded by porridge in winter. Lunchtimes are soup, homemade bread rolls with different fillings, and fruit salad, and for tea we have a small main meal followed by a small dessert.

Another important shift in our eating habits generated by our new lifestyle was the realization that we could adapt our diet to fit what we grew and what was available locally.

For example, Geoff makes fresh soup every few days from whatever we have in the garden and whatever needs using up. Into a vegetable soup goes, say, parsnips or carrots from the garden, a stalk of the cauliflower or broccoli we have bought from the shop, and half a home-grown potato. When processed and enhanced with homemade seasonings and garden herbs this provides a delicious starter for a few cents. If we have a glut of tomatoes, onions, or artichokes, these form the basis of our soups.

In Wales, we made jam from blackcurrants from the garden and locally foraged blackberries. But blackcurrants and blueberries don't like the warmth of our Portuguese garden and we never have a surplus of strawberries for jams. But what we do have is a lime tree that is laden down with fruit every year. From the fruit, Geoff makes about thirty jars each year of wonderfully tangy lime marmalade, which we have on our breakfast rolls. Since imported English marmalade is expensive, at about eight euros a jar, this is a valuable addition to our larder.

Our lime tree certainly pays its way. As well as marmalade and as many fresh limes as we can eat, it also provides enough fruit for lime pickle, which Geoff makes using traditional fermentation methods. In the UK, having to go out to work meant it was difficult to make fermented foods as they require daily attention. During the first part of the fermentation process, the lids of storage jars must be lifted once or twice daily to allow the gases to escape. Naturally fermented foods are not only delicious, they also contain lots of beneficial bacteria so are thought to be important for gut health and general well-being. Unfortunately, because they are live, they cannot be easily stored and transported outside of the home, which is why you will not often find them on supermarket shelves.

Fermentation is one of the oldest methods of preserving

all sorts of foods, from vegetables to fish. But it is easy to see why vinegar began to be used in foods that were traditionally fermented. For example, foods like sauerkraut, mustard, pickles, and chutneys are today preserved in vinegar instead of fermented to ensure a long shelf life. This means they are no longer live foods. Ironically, they can also be expensive.

To preserve our garden produce Geoff fermented our surplus cucumbers, radish, tomatoes, garlic, and carrots. As well as the lime pickle, he made kombucha, ginger beer, and apple cider vinegar. When it became increasingly difficult to find natural live yoghurt at a decent price, we bought a cheap yoghurt maker. Now, every ten days, I make seven jars of live yoghurt. Mixing a few spoonfuls of yoghurt from a previous batch with a litre of UHT milk takes only ten minutes; the yoghurt maker does the rest.

In Wales, we had tried to grow a grapevine in our polytunnel but the poor thing coped badly with the freezing temperatures. In our Portuguese garden, we had three grapevines and were determined to make full use of them. Geoff made red, white, and rose wine, and we stuffed the delicious young vine leaves with rice and vegetables.

Our nasturtium plants proliferated in the warm climate and one day, puzzling over a good way to use the abundance of leaves, Geoff hit upon the idea of making fresh pesto with them. We loved pesto, but good quality pesto was both expensive and difficult to find. We discovered that processed nasturtium leaves, mixed with good olive oil, cheese, garlic, and toasted Brazil or cashew nuts make an outstanding pesto. Geoff now makes several batches a year and freezes it so we have a constant supply.

It was all very well having our own fruit and vegetables but now that we had stopped eating meat and fish and returned to a vegetarian diet, we needed a decent source of protein. Of course we ate plenty of beans and pulses, but we also liked more textured products like veggie burgers. Vegetarian products made from soy beans and other plant-based ingredients were available from the local supermarkets, but they tended to be heavily preserved, fairly tasteless, and rather expensive. So Geoff made his own burgers and sausages from recipes he developed, using high gluten flour, eggs, and beans. Another food we liked was fresh tofu, but this was both hard to find and pricey, so we bought soy beans and started making it from scratch.

After toying with the idea of getting a few chickens, we finally concluded that we didn't have enough space to give them anything like a normal life, so we continued buying local eggs from Mrs Costa. Cheese was a different matter. We are both cheese addicts. Although we liked the many varieties of Portuguese cheese we hankered after British cheese; the tangy sharpness of hard Cheshire and Cheddar cheeses, and the salty creaminess of Caerphilly. By the time we left the UK, the full-flavoured locally produced cheeses we remembered from childhood were becoming increasingly difficult to find. In Portugal, they were almost impossible to source.

We did eventually find a supply of (expensive) Stilton but we noticed that after a few days in the fridge it started to become oily. And we found that other commercial cheese we bought sometimes didn't behave as expected. Despite careful storage, the Parmesan cheese we bought for cooking quickly went mouldy. Disheartened, Geoff practically stopped eating cheese. Such is my cheese addiction that I persisted with the poor quality Cheddar available at the supermarket, but we finally gave up on that. After doing some research, Geoff decided to try his hand at cheese-making.

We invested in a cheese press, some cheesecloth, and a few different types of cheese cultures. To mimic the dry coolness of a cheese 'cave' we bought a cheap wine fridge. We found that making cheese is not that difficult, but it takes time and one has to respond sensitively to the vagaries of each different mixture. Geoff adapted recipes according to the season and how the mixture responded on a given day; like the ferments, home-produced cheese is more alive and less standardized than the factory-made equivalent.

Once the milk has been heated and the cultures and other ingredients added, the curds must be left to drain and then separated from the whey. Then the cheese must be pressed. Hard cheeses like Cheddar and Double Gloucester are best matured for a few months before eating. To ensure we always have a ready supply of cheese, Geoff also makes Caerphilly, which is ready to eat in only three weeks, and soft cheese flavoured with home-grown garlic and parsley. The soft cheese can be made with UHT milk and can be eaten immediately. Our homemade cheese must be tasted to be believed. It is like no cheese either of us has eaten before.

The success of the cheese prompted Geoff to try his hand at replacing other foods we had always bought with artisan versions. He developed recipes for a whole range of staples, from cat food to condiments. Our meals were now enriched with homemade seasonings, sauces, and dressings. As well as making mustard and pesto, he made fresh ketchups and relishes, chutneys for longer term storage, and large bottles of sweet chilli sauce from our own chillies.

Some of these foods we had stopped buying because we weren't keen on the amount of preservatives, colourings, and other artificial ingredients they contained. Others were expensive, so we deliberately limited ourselves to buying them only occasionally. But the homemade versions Geoff made were so much tastier and cheaper that we were able to eat them whenever we liked.

For example, we both love tahini. We had found a supply of this tasty sesame paste in a specialist supermarket in Porto. But at nearly five euros for a small jar, it was woefully expensive, and at times it had a distinct scent of peanuts. We suspected that the manufacturers were adding other ingredients to cheapen it. Sesame seeds are relatively inexpensive to buy in bulk online. Toasted, ground up, and mixed with olive oil and a little salt, they make a fantastically rich tahini. Geoff made large boxes of the stuff for less than we had previously paid for a small jar.

In the UK, I had occasionally treated myself to a small jar of cashew nut butter. We considered organic nut butters another pricey luxury, if they could be found. After his success with the tahini, Geoff experimented with nut butter recipes. The one he finally came up with is delicious, and consists (depending on which of these we have in) of processed almonds, walnuts, cashews, sunflower seeds, sesame seeds, and chia seeds, mixed with olive oil and a little honey to sweeten.

Being able to eat expensive foods like nut butters and high-quality cheese whenever we want to rather than only when we can afford them has undoubtedly upped our quality of life. But it has also taught us an important lesson: money doesn't necessarily buy quality. The fact is that if we were ten times richer than we are now, we still wouldn't be able to buy food that tastes as good as Geoff's homemade equivalent. Food that is home-grown or locally grown and made fresh always tastes better (and is better for you).

Eating well is as basic as breathing. The person who doesn't eat well is not living well. We have come to realize that having the time to devote to growing and preparing food at home is probably the biggest way in which we have improved our quality of life since moving to Portugal. And in the increasingly uncertain world we now find ourselves in, we feel that having a homestead (no matter how small) to support and nourish you is essential to health and well-being.

17

At the beginning of the sitcom *The Good Life*, Tom Good puzzles over how to find 'It', the sense of meaning that seems absent from his well-paid but rather pointless job designing the little plastic models that come with packets of cereal. Hungry for a more fulfilling life, Tom's solution was to give up all forms of paid work and become completely self-sufficient. Our own solution was different. Unlike Tom, we had no wish to spend our days tending pigs or weaving. We wanted a modest, simple, sustainable way of life that allowed us time for writing and self-development.

We had discovered that it is easier said than done to extricate yourself completely from the system, especially if it is just the two of you (as opposed to a community). Even on our remote hillside in Wales, with plenty of space and an off-grid system, the weather limited the range of food we could grow and we were still dependent on our city jobs to provide the money to pay for fuel and fund the renovation of the house. At the time, it had felt like a compromise. However, in hindsight, we had learnt a valuable lesson: our purist vision of rejecting the system and living in the middle of nowhere had its own costs.

It is all very well being off-grid if you can afford a large solar set-up with lots of panels and batteries and maybe some wind and hydro power as backup. If not, then you must be prepared to do without a washing machine, fridge, freezer, and an Internet connection. Unless you are fortunate enough to have your own small woodland, logs and coal must be bought in. In Wales, our primitive hillside cottage with its wild, exposed garden and tiny off-grid system was never going to be an independent smallholding. In Portugal, our plot of land was smaller still; smallholdings within the city boundaries, though available, did not come cheap. As in Wales, we were compromising.

However, we were realizing that there was more than one type of self-sufficiency. In trying to carve out a sustainable lifestyle in the city, we had been inspired by the idea of 'urban homesteading', an approach developed in the United States by Jules Dervaes, amongst others. Keen to try and feed his family from the backyard of his suburban home in California, Dervaes had realized that he didn't need to move out of the city and buy more land to grow food. Instead, he used every square inch of his modest plot to create a verdant, productive garden that not only provided food for his large family but produced a surplus that he could sell.

We liked Dervaes' philosophy; he recognized that it can be more sustainable to live in the city and on the system, and grow intensively in a small space. He also emphasized the importance of relocating work, food production, leisure, and many other activities back to the home, rather than relying on outside sources.

In developing our own homestead, Geoff was naturally following many of the urban homesteading principles: using every viable part of the garden to grow edibles organically, replanting quickly when a plant had been harvested, growing foods that we ate the most and that were most expensive to buy, preserving food, and growing and cooking frugally and wisely, so that little was wasted. Our pretty potager provided us with a wide variety of food in amounts we could use. We needed lots of different types of foods, rather than one or two monocultures. A field of potatoes and rows and rows of cabbages would have been no good to us. Instead, we needed small amounts of choice varieties that could be picked fresh: cut-and-come-again salad leaves, fresh herbs, a handful of new potatoes here and there.

In leaving North Wales and moving to Porto, we had returned to the city and embraced some of the trappings of modernity that we had rejected in the UK. Although our immediate neighbourhood was like a small village in many ways, we were firmly within the city boundaries and back on mains water and electricity. But we were finding out that living a more independent, authentic life was about more than being physically off-system. It wasn't as simple as just finding off-system ways to replace on-system processes. Rather, it was about questioning the system and developing alternative strategies that could lead to a greater sense of fulfilment and connection.

Jules Dervaes insisted that growing your own food is itself an act of resistance, a kind of backyard revolution. Nowadays, food production and distribution is mostly under the control of large multinational corporations. As I write, the effects of global inflation, climate change, and the recent COVID-19 pandemic have pushed food prices up alarmingly. Governments and corporations are increasingly keen to curate the type of food we eat. As most of us are dependent on food that is not produced in our own locale, we have little control over the quantity and quality of the food available to us. The seemingly simple decision to grow your own food can't provide immunity from the effects of a crazy world, but it can help to regain some control over what is arguably the thing that most affects your quality of life: the food that you put into your mouth each day.

Growing a few greens may not sound radical but it is. Producing some of your own food, whether in a garden or on an allotment or balcony, is a fundamental act of disengaging from the agenda of centralized food production, which is often distorted by considerations of money and power, and rediscovering the connection to more local sources of nourishment. It involves reclaiming responsibility for your own health and well-being rather than being totally dependent on outside forces.

For us, developing our city garden demanded a shift in attitude. Maybe we didn't have to run away to some remote countryside hideout to be more self-reliant and find contentment. Maybe it was all about what Dervaes called 'adapting in place'; tailoring homesteading principles to the city environment, rewilding the urban jungle.

We discovered that there were many advantages to homesteading in the city. Maybe we couldn't grow all our own food on our small plot, but there were shops within walking distance where we could buy locally produced fruit, vegetables, and eggs. We had plenty of neighbours who we could swap plants and produce with, and there were many small producers in Portugal who were happy to deliver supplies if you plucked up enough courage to try out your Portuguese in email or phone conversations.

For instance, we found a wonderful family farm in the Trás-os-Montes region that produced olive oil and mountain honey and delivered to customers in Porto. Now, every year, we buy large amounts of both from the farm, as well as fresh walnuts and organic wine. An Internet search turned up a traditional dried goods supplier in Lisbon, from whom we buy most of our dried fruits and nuts. We are constantly on the lookout for new local producers.

In the UK, our remote location meant that prepping on food and other supplies was essential. Because Geoff cooks from scratch, we keep in stock good supplies of basic ingredients like flour, beans, nuts, and seeds. Browsing in a second-hand shop in Porto one day, we came across an old pine cupboard, the top half of which had glass doors and shelves. It was perfect for our kitchen and is now full of glass jars containing dried fruit, beans and pulses, and nuts.

After we renovated our small cellar, we began prepping in earnest. For some reason, we have both always been enamoured of root cellars and larders, from the images of the cellars and storehouses of Amish homes, with their orderly rows of home-grown and home-preserved produce, to the accounts of larders and pantries in literature. I loved reading the description of Bilbo Baggins' snug underground hobbit hole with its labyrinthine corridors, cupboards, and larder. The first time I saw Jill Barklem's beautiful drawings of the mice of Brambly Hedge, I was captivated by her depictions of their homey kitchens and storerooms, usually situated in a cosy underground burrow or tree stump. These idyllic spaces are crammed with boxes of apples and jars and crocks of delicious sounding goods like sugared violets and caraway biscuits, and festooned with hanging bunches of herbs. And who could resist Shirley Jackson's account of the shining jars of Constance's pantry in the castle, an image of rosy domesticity that (because this is Jackson) is not all it seems.

We fitted our own cellar with shelves which we filled with tinned tomatoes and fruit to see us through the winter months, jars of honey, five litre bottles of olive oil, and packets of ground coffee and tea. Jars of Geoff's marmalade gave off a rich golden glow and reminded us of summer. Fat homemade cheeses filled the 'cheese cave' and bottles of home-produced wine and beer clustered in every available corner. We acquired some large plastic tubs and filled them with bags of flour, sugar, and spices. We devoted a couple of shelves to non-food products and stocked them with bars of soap, dishwashing liquid, shampoo, and toothpaste.

We stocked the cellar gradually and shopped strategically, doubling up on purchases if a particular product was reduced and buying in bulk when funds allowed. In this way, we managed to build up a supply of food and other essentials that would realistically last us for about two years. What this means is that we don't need to worry as much if, for reasons of illness, unemployment, or just bad weather, we cannot do our weekly shop. In these times of rising inflation and food shortages, having a modest prep pantry has been invaluable.

In truth, our pantry has been a blessing over the last twelve months. Almost a year ago to the day, I managed to badly break my arm, necessitating several months off work. With only one good hand, I was unable to do any copyediting so our income dropped dramatically. The fact that we live on very little and produce so much of our own food (and have a well-stocked prep store) meant that this unexpected event was not quite the disaster it might have been. In fact, the period of forced inactivity proved valuable in other ways. It gave us a chance to reflect on the experiences described here, and recovering from surgery on my arm, I began writing (one-handedly at first!) *Escape to the Hills*.

Although we used traditional methods such as fermentation to preserve many foods, being back on the system meant that for the first time in years we were able to run a small chest freezer. In this, we stored surplus garden produce, such as bags of green beans and cherry tomatoes, and boxes of soup, custard, sauces, and other foods that Geoff had batch-cooked and which could be de-frozen on a busy day.

Our city location was ideal in another important respect. Even though our finances had improved, we resisted buying a car. With shops, cafes, and bus stops within easy walking distance and no need to travel to a workplace, we couldn't really justify the considerable expense of a car. Besides, we had had enough of all that. In the UK, our remote hillside location meant that having a reliable car was a must, and we spent thousands on fuel and car maintenance. We were reluctant to return to the hassle and expense of keeping a vehicle. Most of our neighbours managed perfectly well without one. In fact, we had noticed an interesting pattern. Most of our older neighbours, like Beatriz and Matilde, didn't have cars and therefore walked most places. They tackled the steep lanes in our neighbourhood with ease. Car ownership was higher amongst our younger neighbours, many of whom struggled on the occasions when they had to climb the hill to reach the bus stop. We knew which role model we preferred.

We watched a video recently by Peter Adeney (aka 'Mr Money Mustache'), the American financial guru who promotes frugal living and financial independence. He made the interesting point that less technical solutions to daily tasks are often cheaper and healthier. For example, eating home-cooked food rather than takeaways, using a manual lawnmower instead of an electric one, walking or cycling rather than using a car — all these are low-cost options that are also better for your health.

We began to feel that living without a car was in many

ways easier. If we needed to be somewhere specific early in the morning, such as with hospital appointments, we simply booked Manuel the taxi driver. This took the strain out of the journey and cut down on the stress of travelling. At least, sometimes it did.

One memorable day, after a hospital appointment in Porto, we caught a taxi. It had been a tiring morning and we just wanted to get home quickly. The elderly taxi driver looked a little worried about the prospect of two *estrangeiros* as passengers but seemed happy enough after we had given him directions. It was a beautiful sunny day and we set off towards the river. However, instead of crossing the bridge over to Gaia, the taxi headed for the river road on Porto side.

Soon we were speeding along a narrow road that hugged the river. The driver seemed confident about where he was going, even if he was taking the hairpin bends rather fast for our liking. For a while, we sat back and enjoyed the views; we had never been down that particular road before and it was interesting to gaze at our neighbourhood from the other side of the water. But soon we grew uneasy. There seemed to be no sign of a bridge.

'You know,' I muttered to Geoff, ' I think the last bridge over to Gaia side was miles back.'

'Are you sure?' he said. 'Well, where is he taking us?'

I tried to visualize our map of the area, which showed the course of the river.

'Um, Spain, I think. At this speed, we should be there soon!'

With difficulty, we persuaded the driver to stop and tried to explain again where we wished to go. When we insisted that we were on the wrong side of the river he threw up his hands in despair and looked glumly across the water, as if trying to conjure up a bridge out of thin air. We eventually persuaded him to go back the way he had come and then proceeded to direct him at every single junction. We still have no idea where he thought he was taking us or why he was so confused about the route. Maybe he had just had a long day.

Most of the time, however, we managed perfectly well with taxis and buses. In one respect though, we missed having our own transport. We often went for walks to explore the local area. But the steep hills limited the distance we could cover. It was easy, for instance, to walk down to the river and follow the coastal path for a couple of miles, stopping off at a cafe to admire the view over a coffee or beer. The walk back up the hill, however, was punishing and had to be tackled slowly, especially on hot summer days. This meant we had to be careful how far we walked because we had to allow substantial time and energy for the return journey.

We reasoned that if we had some mode of transport we could cover more ground. The obvious low-cost solution was to acquire bicycles. However, we had seen the hardened mountain bikers who sometimes whizzed down our lane on their way to the river dismount at the bottom of our steep lanes to push their bikes resignedly up the hills. Not an enticing prospect. Then, we hit upon the perfect vehicle for our terrain; the electric bike. We did some research and bought two foldable electric bikes in a seasonal sale.

Neither of us had cycled for many years, but a first experimental lap around the neighbourhood reassured us that our new mode of transport would be fast and fun. We waved to an open-mouthed Beatriz as we sailed past her house. Later that day, she called round to apologize for not waving back. She hadn't recognized us she said. She thought the bikes were marvellous and weren't we fit to be able to cycle so quickly up those hills! I smiled modestly and decided not to confess just yet about the bikes being electric. It wouldn't do any harm to bask for a few days in our new reputation for being super fit.

The bikes broadened our local horizons considerably. As well as visiting our favourite haunts down by the river we explored further afield, cycling down the quiet lanes further inland. The bikes allowed access to areas we would never have discovered by car; we happened upon secluded little stretches of woodland, ancient tracks and alleyways, and old abandoned *quintas* lying half-hidden behind tumbledown walls.

One day, we braved the tiny alleys and steps that led down to one of the small tributaries that flow into the River Douro. This was a whole different world. Here, time seemed to have stood still. Tiny crooked houses flanked the steep cobbled alleys, which were populated by groups of stray cats. Laundry flapped above these shady thoroughfares, and the smells of cooking drifted on the breeze. Picking our way down these lanes towards the river, we received a mixture of smiles and stares; the inhabitants of these ancient neighbourhoods rarely saw any through traffic.

On our way back, we left the residents of the alleyways in peace and chose a different route past an old windmill. The ride was pleasant, and we dawdled down sheltered lanes flanked by tall hedgerows until, rounding a corner, the view opened up before us. To the left of the road was a broad field that led down to the river, and a row of pastel-coloured cottages. A few contented-looking sheep and goats were grazing in the sunshine. Enticed by the charming view, we stopped and leant the bikes up against the wall, listening to the soft tinkling from the goat bells.

The view on the opposite side of the road was equally bucolic. In another large field, a few horses were ambling about. Towards the far end of the field, the land sloped upwards and turned into lush woodland. It was an idyllic scene, and we left it reluctantly to continue our journey.

Having a mode of transport, albeit a simple one, wasn't just useful for leisure, it also provided a low-cost independent means of travel (within reason) if we had to go further afield to shop, and meant we could save on bus and taxi fares.

In areas other than transport, we were keen to see how much we could do independently while living within the constraints of the system. For example, even though we now had mains electricity, we had had a small solar array installed during the initial building work on the house. This had been arranged by our builder, Jorge, who had located a company that installed solar panels and controllers. Our modest set-up fed into the mains supply and helped to offset our electricity usage. However, what we hadn't realized at the time was that this system wasn't entirely legit. Much later, we found out that because our system fed into the mains, we should have applied for some kind of licence to install it. The man who had installed our solar set-up had in fact provided us with a guerrilla system, not an uncommon practice in Portugal.

Never entirely comfortable with our rather dodgy system, when the solar controller developed problems we took the opportunity of changing it. We bought a new controller and some heavy duty batteries and Geoff rewired the panels so that instead of feeding into the mains system, our solar set-up functioned as an independent UPS, an uninterruptible power supply.

While it was useful in many ways to have mains power, in some respects it was a pain in the neck. The Portuguese electricity infrastructure seems as sensitive to bad weather as do the country's inhabitants. Inclement weather brought out the worst in our neighbours. Those with normally sunny dispositions became morose and grumpy after a few days of rain or a cold snap, and those who were by nature more melancholy closed their shutters and sulked until the sun came out again. Likewise, when the weather turned troublesome, the power supply became increasingly unstable. The kind of wet, windy weather that in Wales we would have considered unremarkable was enough to take out the fragile infrastructure of our local power station.

Perhaps because of the vagaries of the power supply, many of our neighbours cooked on calor gas. Some even had battery-powered lights, as we soon found out during our first power cut. On that occasion, a huge electrical storm had taken out the system. It was dusk and the few street lights that had winked on promptly winked off again. We looked out across the lane to see various of our neighbours standing on their balconies and terraces trying to work out if it was just their own lights that had gone out or if everyone was affected. Most houses were in darkness but we were surprised to see a bright light from Beatriz' upper floor. Then my phone rang out: it was Beatriz, calling to see if we had enough candles. I assured her that we had and expressed surprise that her own house wasn't affected. She told me that as well as a stock of candles she had several battery-powered lanterns that she kept for just these occasions.

If I had an editing deadline and the weather turned nasty, I knew I had to speed up. Fingers flying over the keyboard, I would race to finish the work before the inevitable power cut. On more than one occasion, Geoff would hear howls from my office as the power cut out and my computer went dead in the middle of a large assignment. Often the power would be restored quickly, but would fail again just as I had recovered all my documents and started work again.

An unexpected power cut was equally inconvenient if

Geoff was particularly busy in the kitchen that day, making cheese for instance, or baking bread. And in the winter the power cuts could occur daily. We needed a solution and the UPS provided it. Geoff ran the wiring through the sitting room, kitchen, and offices, and also installed some low wattage LED lights. The stereo, sitting room lights, and computers now ran off our own UPS system. This meant that in the event of a power cut, we didn't need to fumble around for candles, and we could continue to work on the computers and charge phones and laptops. In fact, during one power cut, we were blissfully unaware of the outage for nearly an hour because our own system was running the computers, music system, and several lights.

Larger appliances like the oven and kettle were too power-hungry for our little system so we found a small counter-top oven/toaster and a low-powered travel kettle. This gave us the best of both worlds. We had the convenience of mains power for most of the time but we now had an alternative system in the event of problems with the mains system.

Our years of living on a remote Welsh hillside had taught us the importance of not being dependent on any one system for essentials. Having a modest UPS and not being totally reliant on others for power made us feel more self-sufficient. As extra insurance, we bought two portable, rechargeable power sources so that we could run other appliances, like the freezer, if we had to. We didn't intend to lose all our surplus food just because of the inefficiencies of the electricity system.

When we lived in our Welsh cottage, we had taken our water supply for granted. The soft spring water we used for drinking and washing was excellent quality and was always available. It was true that we had to take responsibility for keeping access to the spring clean and for pumping the water up to the house but at the end of the day, our water supply was completely under our control. When we were house-hunting in Porto, it hadn't occurred to us to look for a house near a spring but in hindsight it was one of the best features of our new neighbourhood. In a curious echo of our former life in the wilderness, we again found ourselves looking after, and depending on, a natural spring.

Although we had mains water too, the water system was as temperamental as the national grid. Our neighbourhood was very old and access was difficult. The combined effects of the aging drainage system and the plethora of underground springs in the area meant that problems were frequent and the local water supply was sometimes cut off with little warning for repairs to be carried out. But luckily, as with the power, we had an alternative supply. We always had several ten litre bottles full of spring water in the house, to feed into our filter. If the mains water was off for a day we simply popped down to the spring to collect more.

Ancient springs such as our own are a precious resource in a hot country like Portugal, and many are still in use today. However, they are sometimes neglected by local councils. Our proximity to the spring and our experience in Wales meant that we fell naturally into the role of looking after the 'spirit of the spring'.

The truth was, the spring was more than a convenient extra source of water. The pennywort and wild geranium tumbling over the old stones, the play of sunlight on the water, the gentle, ever-present sound of the water trickling through the stone runnels and dripping into mossy hollows created a tiny sanctuary, a quiet shady refuge from the bustle of the neighbourhood.

Sometimes when you went down to the spring on a calm, still day, you might hear a quiet voice, just within hearing range. Spinning round, there would be nobody there. Or there might be the hint of movement, a shadow seen out of the corner of your eye. We experienced the same sensations near the spring on our Welsh hillside. Perhaps the water spirits of these ancient places get lonely sometimes and like a little company.

The spring looked after the local wildlife as well the local people. The sparrows and blackbirds sat in the elder tree that grew above the water source, flying down to take their baths in the little pools beneath. Snails cosied into the mossy corners and spiders laced the stone edifice with large webs that sparkled with water droplets. If you were lucky, you might see a dragonfly or two down there, shimmering briefly above the water before flitting rapidly away like shy fairies.

One day, Geoff went down to collect water and was surprised to see that the flow had slowed considerably despite the recent heavy rain showers. But interestingly, he could see water seeping between the joints of the stonework of the edifice. Obviously, the water was building up but couldn't escape quickly enough. Tentatively, he put his hand inside the little tunnel from which the water flowed and fished around. His hand touched upon what felt like a bit of knobbly wood, and he pulled hard. It was a large elder root that had obviously found its way into the water channel. Now the channel was suddenly clear, the water gushed out with force, rather alarming Matilde, who was down there doing her laundry. Geoff showed her the root and she grinned toothlessly and marvelled at the culprit.

Geoff spent the rest of the morning brushing up excess water and making sure that all the other channels were clear, while Matilde kept up a running commentary on his progress. But if we thought that things would be quiet at the spring for a while, we were mistaken. Just a few days later, when I went down to collect water, we came across another little spirit of the place who was soon to have a big impact on our lives.

18

Bent over the spring outlet with my water carrier, I had a definite sense of being watched. I spun round. Nothing. But the sensation persisted. I finished at the spring and started the journey back up the steps. Suddenly, I saw a little face peering up at me from a dusty corner near the steps. I put down the water carrier and went closer. There, almost camouflaged by the grey and white of the stone, was a small scruffy cat. Its long fur was a dirty yellow-white with grey splotches. It had a small pinched face with hardly any whiskers to speak of. A pair of beautiful amber eyes gazed up at me solemnly, and when I spoke gently to it, it didn't run away.

I returned to the house and told Geoff.

'Funny,' he said. 'I had a dream about a cat last night.'

'What happened?'

'Well — it was odd really — there was this woman, she had blond hair, but big, you know, all piled up on her head, and she was in a kind of luminous dress. She walked up to me and put her arms round me. Then she said "You need me."'

'Weird,' I said.

'Then I looked down and there was a cat round her feet,

a grey and white one, like a Persian or something.'

'Seriously?'

'Yes. Why?'

'That cat down at the spring … it's a grey and white Persian.'

He looked at me. 'Show me.'

We went down to inspect the cat. It was still huddled in its corner.

'It looks like a male,' I said. 'A very old male.'

'It doesn't look well,' Geoff said.

'Maybe we should give it some food.'

'Best not,' Geoff said. 'It might just be disoriented or tired. It might be on its way home.'

But the next day, the cat was still there. We took it some cat food. It wolfed the food then cried piteously for more. We fed her (I had been wrong about it being a male) for the next two days and asked around the neighbourhood to see if anyone had lost a cat. Nobody had. Although nervous of us, the cat wasn't completely wild so had obviously been owned at some point. But she was in a shocking state. Her long fur was heavily matted and her whiskers were very short, as if they had been cut. She looked bone tired, and her little face wore a worried expression, as if she had the weight of the whole world on her shoulders.

After three days, she showed no signs of leaving the spring, so we decided to adopt her. Bibby had died two years previously and we hadn't had the heart to try and replace him. But this little stray was surely a soul in distress, and we knew she wouldn't survive if left on the street.

So Leeloo, as we named her, moved in. Maybe it was Geoff's curious dream, but we always felt that in many ways she was more than a cat. For one thing, she was neurotic as hell. Leeloo's various hang-ups became apparent in the first few weeks. At first, she wouldn't eat if we were anywhere near her. She would stand over her food bowl, monitoring us out of the corner of her eye until we left her in peace. She also had an obsession with steps. In the garden, she would only sit or sleep on a step, never on flat ground. It was the same in the house. In time, we persuaded her to sleep in other locations but she chose these carefully. For instance, if it was cold, she would sleep on the rug in front of the fire rather than on the stairs, but only on the very edge of the rug; in other words, only on the bit that visually resembled the edge of a step.

We also discovered that Leeloo had a talent for falling off things. Only four weeks after she had moved in, she fell off the terrace, tumbling twenty feet down into the valley. She had dozed off in the sunshine near the edge of the terrace. We hadn't thought to move her; after all, cats have a natural grace and a good head for heights don't they? Not this one. The first we knew of her accident was when Maria knocked at the gate. Was this our cat? Maria had found her back down at the spring. Leeloo seemed a little dazed but none the worse for wear.

Her general nervousness, poor condition, and malnourished appearance suggested that Leeloo had not been treated well before she came to us. Beneath her thick coat she was painfully thin. And the coat was in an awful state. We thought at first that she had joint problems in her back legs because she didn't seem able to stand for more than a few seconds. But we soon realized that it was the extensive mats in her fur that were restricting her movements. The process of removing the mats and restoring her skin to a reasonable condition was a slow one. It took even longer before she began to put on weight and lost her rather haunted expression.

As Leeloo's health improved, we realized that far from

being the old cat we had first taken her for, she was in fact quite young. It was clear that her earlier experiences had affected her badly. We could only hope that our care was going some way towards healing the physical and psychological scars she had.

She was certainly enjoying all the attention we lavished on her. In addition to lots of grooming care, we had to work hard on her diet. Leeloo's delicate system responded poorly to commercial cat food so we switched her to human grade chicken and fish, supplemented with cat biscuits. We were concerned when we noticed her licking the garden paths, and assumed she had a mineral deficiency. But as we got to know her better we realized that she licked any surface — cement, carpet, tiles — only when she was nervous, which initially was most of the time. Although she is now more relaxed, she still occasionally scratches or licks the floor if she is nervous about communicating her intentions to us.

Of all the cats we have lived with, Leeloo is the one that has needed the most care. After spending a morning giving Leeloo a bath followed by cooking chicken for her, Geoff said to me, 'Do you know that dream I had of Leeloo and the woman?'

'Yes.'

'Well the woman — let's assume she was Leeloo's spirit or guardian angel or something — said "You need me."'

'So?'

'Well, God knows why she thought I needed Leeloo; the little minx causes me huge amounts of bloody trouble!'

But Geoff was joking. The little soul we rescued is the most sweet-natured and loving of animals; just her presence has repaid us amply for all the care she has received.

About a year after we adopted Leeloo, Geoff happened to see a picture of Marie Antoinette on the Internet.

'My God,' he said. 'Look at this.'

‘What?’

‘That’s the woman in my dream! The one with the cat.’

Curiously, we subsequently read that Persian cats roamed the palace at Versailles, and that Louis XV had a favourite white Persian cat that he doted on. We like to joke that Leeloo is a reincarnation of Marie Antoinette; she certainly has an air of royalty about her, treats us like servants, and loves cake. Now one of her many nicknames is ‘Furry Antoinette.’

More recently, we have been intrigued at the number of cultural references to Marie Antoinette. It seems that everywhere you look, there are new books, films, and cultural memes about the eighteenth-century French queen. In these times of global unrest, references to the French revolution seem strangely apt.

For the arrival of Leeloo wasn’t the only sign of change in our little backwater. The rhythms of the people, animals, and weather were changing, and these changes were apparent in the new patterns of the orrery we observed from our windows.

For one thing, the weather was definitely changing. We moved to our Welsh cottage in 1999, and for the first few years there the weather was warm, even in our elevated location in the mountains. We congratulated ourselves on moving to the mountains; if the climate was going to heat up then at least we had water and a cooler environment. But as the weather in the UK steadily worsened and the winters grew colder and colder, our thoughts had turned to sunnier climes. Now we are glad we chose Portugal as our new home. It is a good place to be in these times of extreme weather changes.

However, we have noticed that even here the weather has grown harsher over the last few years. The winters are much colder than they were; sometimes we even see frost on the surrounding rooftops. The exotic palm trees that we so admired when we first moved here are slowly disappearing and the rain showers are more torrential. The biting wind that drove us from our Welsh hillside has followed us; it is getting harder to grow warmer weather plants like tomatoes and peppers. In our first years here, the sound of cicadas was a constant accompaniment on summer nights but now we hardly ever hear them.

In our earlier years here, we would sometimes see wild parrots perched in trees in Porto city centre, a sign of balmier weather. Nowadays the parrots have disappeared and we have more temperate weather visitors to the garden; robins, blackbirds, and magpies. One of our most frequent visitors is a male blackbird with one white feather and a white splodge on his head, who we have nicknamed Albie. While the human inhabitants of the neighbourhood may not be keen on the wetter weather that is becoming the norm, Albie loves his morning forays on the damp garden beds, where he will spend a good hour tossing leaves aside (usually onto the garden paths) in his search for worms and woodlice.

In 2022, after a period of heavy rainfall, a small landslide occurred when the garden wall of a nearby house collapsed, taking a portion of the road with it. This house was occupied by a family we called the Novo Clampetts. In Liverpool, our next door neighbours the Clampetts, and their replacements the NeoClampetts, had been hard to live with. Having one set of noisy next door neighbours can be considered unlucky, having two sets is perhaps a cruel twist of fate. But three sets must surely be seen as some kind of sign from the universe ... of what we didn't know.

Like our previous Clampett neighbours, the Novo Clampetts were very friendly and we got on well with them. But their almost obsessive car use sometimes drove us half-crazy. Both Senhor and Senhora Clampett had a car each, as did their teenage son and daughter. The complicated work and college schedules of the family meant that at almost any time of the day there was always one car noisily arriving or departing. In a way, the Novo Clampetts provided a kind of half-hourly orrery of their very own.

The landslide that occurred was only partly the fault of the wet weather; the Novo Clampetts didn't believe in house maintenance and their ancient boundary walls were some of the most unstable in the neighbourhood. The local council responded quickly and a team of workmen, or *trolhas*, were soon tackling the job of rebuilding the wall and reconstructing the road. Unfortunately, the *trolha* gang was both noisy and incompetent, and by the time they had restored the road to a semblance of its former structure they had managed to antagonize almost everyone on the lane.

Several times a day, the *trolhas* trundled up and down the lane, moving large amounts of sand and cement in an ancient rickety digger driven with complete abandon. With the small digger, they managed to damage our gutter and knock a chunk out of Alta Man's wall. One day, we had been shopping and returned home to find a small frantic scene unfolding near our gate. A police car was parked in the lane and a weary looking policeman was trying to make notes as his colleague tried to calm Alta Man's daughter Mariazinha, who was shouting and gesticulating wildly towards the *trolhas*, who were standing sullenly on the corner.

It wasn't long before Beatriz and Maria, curious about the noise, had strolled down the lane from their own houses to join in the discussion. We knew for a fact that

Beatriz had phoned both the council and the police several times to complain about what she considered the loutish behaviour of the *trolhas*. It seemed that her phone calls had had some effect. When a few days later the *trolhas* at last finished their work and departed, leaving a trail of minor but irritating destruction behind them, the whole neighbourhood breathed a sigh of relief.

The building work on the lane wasn't the only source of local tension that year. The effects of the COVID-19 pandemic made themselves felt in several ways. The households of some of our older neighbours swelled as relatives who had lost their jobs and found themselves struggling to meet rental or mortgage payments moved back into the family home, sometimes temporarily. The practice of social distancing reduced the amount of neighbourly contact and introduced a new, thankfully temporary, wariness of strangers which we had not seen before.

After a period of ill-health, Mrs Costa announced she was retiring. This was gloomy news indeed. Not only would we miss our weekly chats with this kind-natured lady, it would be sad to see our little local shop disappear. A weekly trudge round a faceless supermarket wouldn't be the same. But a few weeks later Mrs Costa introduced us to Isabel, a cheerful young woman who we learnt had bought the shop and would shortly be taking over. Like many other people in the neighbourhood, we were relieved that our local shop, which has held out for so long against the influx of the supermarkets, would live to fight another day.

And Isabel breathed new life into the shop. She built new attractive displays for the fresh produce and enthusiastically launched weekly campaigns to encourage her customers to sample some of the new lines she stocked. These didn't always prove popular with the older customers. For example, the Halloween decorations she put up a few weeks after taking over the shop met with disapproval from some of the older ladies, who considered Halloween a heathen abomination.

Isabel had lived abroad for ten years and although she told us that she considered Portugal to be home, she struggled with the traditional attitudes of some of the older residents of the neighbourhood. Having been exposed to different cuisines, she was impatient sometimes with the eating habits of some of her customers. One Easter, we asked her if she would be preparing the traditional Easter dish, *cabrito*, cooked lamb. She wrinkled her nose.

'I hate it!' Isabel said, in her excellent English. 'They will all be eating it on Easter Sunday but I will be having a salad!'

'Your spirit isn't Portuguese any more,' Geoff observed. 'It's changed.'

Isabel nodded her head. 'I think it has.'

But Isabel still retained some of the traditional bewilderment when she learnt of our vegetarian diet. Despite being fascinated by some of the foods we ate (she had once tried tofu, for instance, and discovered to her surprise that she really liked it), she looked worried when we told her that no, we didn't eat any meat or fish any more.

'So you just eat vegetables?' she said in wonder.

'Yes, and beans and pulses, and things,' Geoff replied.

'But, but ... can you survive on that?' she asked, reducing us to giggles.

On one of our visits, we had been delighted to find that Isabel had installed a new product display.

'Wow, fresh mushrooms!' I exclaimed. We loved mushrooms but they are not easy to find outside of the supermarkets in Portugal.

'Take as many as you like,' Isabel said gloomily. 'Is only you and me eating them.'

'Why?' Geoff asked. 'Haven't you sold many?'

Isabel raised her eyes to the heavens. 'I tell you,' she said, 'is so hard to convince people to eat them! Oh, wait a minute ... João!'

This latter was delivered to her eight-year-old son who was not in school that day because of a strike and who was spending his holiday lolling about in the doorway playing with a toy plastic axe.

'I wish I hadn't bought him that,' Isabel muttered.

We all gazed at the miscreant in the doorway. Isabel's son was a live wire, highly intelligent and easily bored. He had the loudest voice we had ever heard on a small child; he didn't talk, he bellowed, an effect rather disconcerting given his slight frame.

Isabel continued relating to us her frustrated efforts to convince her older customers of the benefits of fresh mushrooms. 'They say to me, "Ugh, what are these?" I tell them they are just like the tinned ones, but they say "No, no, they are the wrong colour!"'

'They're only a different colour because they're not cooked and the tinned ones are,' Geoff pointed out.

'I know,' said Isabel, 'but they won't believe me! They think they are … what is the word … venomous—'

'—Poisonous.'

'Yes, poisonous, and they say to me, "What are you trying to do, poison us?" I say to them, "Yes, yes, of course, I am trying to kill all my customers"'!

She flung her hands up in the air in exasperation.

'Maybe you should set up one of your displays,' I suggested. 'Offer samples of mushrooms cooked in butter to people.'

Her eyes lit up as she started to dream up a new campaign. We bid her goodbye and left her to her plotting.

As we were leaving, a cyclist rode leisurely past the shop. Little João let out a deafening yell, startling us all. Brandishing his small axe, the boy grinned and raced after the startled cyclist, who began to wobble alarmingly as he attempted to steer while peering over his shoulder at his small assailant. Isabel flew out of the shop to rescue the cyclist and we made our escape.

We fervently hope that Isabel's shop survives for many years to come. As in most countries, many of the traditional ways of living, such as shopping locally and growing your own food, have started to disappear. We have noticed a distinct generational gap in our own neighbourhood. Our younger neighbours are increasingly reliant on their cars. They rarely walk round the local lanes and they take the car to the supermarket to shop rather than visiting Isabel's. They usually prefer to go out for food rather than grow and cook it themselves, and they wouldn't dream of collecting their drinking water from the spring. In contrast to older generations, they buy everything in rather than trying to produce it themselves.

We recently saw some footage of our parish in the 1950s. The decade is not that long ago, still well within living memory. Yet the grainy black and white footage spoke of a different world. In the little local harbour, fishing boats dotted the water and groups of women sang as they washed clothes on the river beaches. Images of the local school showed the children in boots and hats playing with hoops and garlanding a maypole with flowers. Outside the school and other public buildings, large stone pots crammed with flowers spilled their blooms onto the dusty lanes, which were empty save for the occasional horse and cart. As the novelist L. P. Hartley once said (in 1953, ironically), 'the past is a foreign country'. But it's a country that seems increasingly attractive to many people today.

As in many European cities, gentrification is changing the face of Porto. Its popularity as a tourist destination has meant that some of the rough edges of this lively city are being smoothed out. On one of our first visits, we were strolling along the sea-front road in Foz de Porto when we stumbled across a tiny boathouse, more of a shack really. A tatty sign advertised boat rides across the river to Afurada, a small fishing hamlet on the Gaia side of the river. We tentatively asked how much at the shack, which was staffed by a very elderly lady who appeared to have no teeth.

After a short and rather choppy river crossing, we spent half an hour strolling round Afurada, which seemed to consist of little more than a sleepy row of cottages and a couple of small cafes, before catching the boat back. Now, Afurada boasts a slick new marina and the tiny shack and its elderly inhabitant are long gone.

Similarly, in the last couple of years many of the traditional small restaurants and cafes on the Gaia riverfront opposite Porto have been replaced by smart new establishments. Every time we go down there, another one of the shops or cafes we used to frequent has gone. On Porto side, the sardine sellers in the Praça da Ribeira have gone and the old tenement buildings with their colourful tiles are being bought up by property developers.

We console ourselves with the thought that all cities change and that some changes are necessary. To the extent that such development brings jobs and better amenities to local communities, it can be a good thing.

Thankfully, the changes in our own backwater are occurring at a much slower pace, and some are positive. For instance, although car ownership has increased, some of our younger neighbours have bought bikes instead. We sense a new attitude of frugality: more people are collecting water from the spring to reduce their water bills and there is a greater enthusiasm for vegetable growing. Even the Novo Clampetts have started gardening. Last summer, they filled their garden with young fruit trees. Unfortunately, after planting, they forgot to water them, despite the fact that it was thirty degrees in the shade. Still. I expect Beatriz will give them lots of unasked for gardening advice this summer.

It was the Greek philosopher Heraclitus who said that you cannot step into the same river twice. Change is the root of life. The Portugal that we live in now is in many ways a different country from the one we moved to twelve years ago. But we know that some things will never change. Our neighbourhood orrery will still turn even as the players and rhythms change, the swallows will still return each spring to hunt in the warm breezes over the valley, and the waters of the River Douro will gleam at the sun's touch on their way to the sea.

EPILOGUE

I remember having a conversation many years ago with Jim, a friend of my father's. The man was a bus driver and he was remarking on my enrolling for a PhD.

'I did a PhD once,' he said.

'Really?' I asked. 'What was your subject?'

'Nuclear physics,' he said.

'So you used to be a physicist once?' I said.

'No. I've always been a bus driver.'

'But, why did you do a PhD then?'

'Well, I always liked physics and I fancied myself as a bit of a thinker, a bit of a problem-solver. After I finished the PhD, my supervisor encouraged me to apply for a research position in a university. And then it dawned on me. I was going to become just like him. I'd be working all hours; I'd have grant proposals to write, PhD students of my own to look after, conferences to go to. I wouldn't be in control of my own time any more. I'd have no time to think. So I became a bus driver.'

'I don't understand. Why a bus driver?'

'Because sitting there driving all day gives me lots of time to think my own thoughts. And that makes me happy.'

At the time, I thought that Jim was a little mad to turn

down an academic career to drive a bus. Now I think I know what he meant. Geoff and I seem always to have been searching for that same kind of peace of mind — for an alternative to the rat race, for a sense of contentment that seems absent from modern life, for that still space in the eye of the storm.

The psychologist Carl Jung believed that the aims and activities of the second half of life should be different from those of the first half. In young adulthood, people are usually preoccupied with such things as establishing a home, finding a partner and perhaps having children, and building a career or finding suitable work. Once past middle age, with those external patterns of life established, the focus should turn inwards. Jung maintained that in later life a person should pay more attention to their inner life, to developing self-understanding, reflecting on their life and coming to terms with the ghosts of the past.

In many ways, this book and its precursor *Escape to the Hills* have been a kind of recapitulation for us both. By writing the books, we have tried to understand the past, to gather together the threads of our personal and shared history in order to make sense of our lives. We need to review where we have been to know where we are, and where we are going.

Reminiscing about our escapes, first to a remote cottage in the Welsh hills and then to the Douro region of Portugal, has helped to make explicit the lessons that have shaped us and the things we have learnt along the way.

At the beginning of our journey we wanted to find an escape route out of modernity, out of the pressures of a society that reifies money, power, and conformity. Rejecting the system, we wanted to be independent and self-reliant. We wanted time to think and to dream, to develop a deeper sense of connection with ourselves and with the world.

Our mistake was to think that we had to run away and find an isolated place to pursue these goals. Twenty years later, we have stopped running. We now realize that being self-sufficient and finding an alternative to the system is not just about having an off-grid set-up or growing organic vegetables. It's not about finding a remote hideaway or dropping out of work. In fact, it's not really about a geographical place at all. True escape is more a mental and emotional attitude.

It is easy to feel in control and at peace if one is halfway up a mountain in a meditation hut. The real trick is to develop strength and peace of mind in the maelstrom of modern life. It is true that our adventures have inculcated a sense of confidence and self-reliance that was absent before. Living with no water or electricity is excellent training for becoming stronger and more flexible. Giving up everything and moving to another country to start a new life forces you out of your normal habits and perceptions and develops a sense of trust in the future.

But we now realize that real self-sufficiency and true peace of mind is not about escaping the world but about finding a new way of being immersed in it. We have learnt the importance of being rooted in the rhythms and seasons of a place, of feeling a part of the place and community in which you live — whether you live in a cottage in the countryside, a bedsit in the city, or follow a more nomadic lifestyle in a van or on a narrowboat.

We have also realized that quality of life is less about money and more about time: time to slow down, to spend time together, to tend a garden, and to prepare and eat good food. These things can't really be bought.

We now understand that we must follow a path that feels authentic and true to us, even if it is daunting and difficult. We know that the alternative, opting for a journey that is more comfortable and predictable, will not in the long term make us happy. As the Buddhists say, it is about the path, not the destination.

For us, finding 'It' has not been about finding a thing or a place. It has been about finding a way of being in the world, of becoming more grounded. The word 'mundane' comes from the Latin *mundus*, the world. It is ironic that in modern times, the word has negative overtones; things or experiences described as 'mundane' are those we consider dull, everyday, or routine — just the sorts of qualities many people dream of escaping from. Nowadays, we feel the opposite. We relish being rooted in our little homestead. We derive energy and satisfaction from focusing down on the small details of our lives: a good meal, the scents of the garden, time spent together. On fine days, we can sometimes see the packed cruise ships glide past our valley on their way downriver. We stand and watch them, wholly content to let them pass us by.

These are stormy times. In political, economic, and climate terms, changes are occurring on a scale most of us have never experienced before. Such times demand a new kind of resilience. A special kind of psychological surefootedness is needed to navigate these waters and thrive in the midst of change and upheaval. This type of resilience comes from within; it must be nurtured by growing the self. When people take more responsibility for their own food, their own well-being, and their own community, this kind of development can take place. We believe that this is the real meaning of self-sufficiency. And it can be practiced anywhere.

Yesterday, I was inspired by the tiny new cherry blossoms appearing in the garden to leaf through one of our books on Japanese gardens. Along with our interest in oriental medicine, Geoff and I both have a weakness for Chinese and Japanese landscapes and gardens.

Even just gazing at the pictures of the sparse, beautifully designed Zen gardens, with their carefully placed rocks, trees, and paths, instilled in me a sense of peace. Zen gardens are intended to invite stillness and contemplation, to provide a serene space in which the meditating mind can try to grasp concepts such as impermanence and eternity.

While I was browsing, Geoff came and looked over my shoulder.

'Look at that,' he said.

The picture he was pointing to was a stunning view of a garden framed by two sliding bamboo screen doors. A Buddhist monk sat in contemplative pose staring out at the scene.

I sighed. 'You know, if we weren't so content here, I think it might be nice to live in Japan.'

'Mmmm,' Geoff said. 'It's funny you should say that. I came across this article, I meant to tell you about it. It was about this village in the mountains of Japan ... amazing place. Well, the article was about this English couple who moved out there. They bought this beautiful traditional wooden house in the village. The villagers all grow their own food, they're self-sufficient in practically everything ...'

I looked at Geoff carefully. He had a strange gleam in his eye.

'Beautiful place,' he said. 'Do you know garlic grows wild in Japan?'

'Are you saying what I think you're saying?' I said.

Geoff smiled, somewhat inscrutably I thought, then said casually, 'Fancy a cup of sencha?'

BIBLIOGRAPHY AND FURTHER READING

Bachelard, G. (1994). *The Poetics of Space* (M. Jolas, Transl.). Beacon Press.

Barklem, J. (2011). *The Complete Brambly Hedge.* HarperCollins

Bell, A. (1912). *In Portugal.* Kessinger Publishing.

Damon, C. (2021). Abandoned wash-houses. Archiving wash-women practices in Oporto modern urban space. *Sophia Journal.* Volume 6, issue 1. https://www.up.pt/revistas/index.php/sophia/article/view/409

Hartley, L. P. (1953). *The Go-Between*. Penguin.

Jackson, S. (2009). *We Have Always Lived in the Castle*. Penguin.

Jung, C. (1989). *Memories, Dreams, Reflections*. Vintage.

Proust, M. (1913/2002). *In Search of Lost Time. Volume One: Swann's Way*. (Lydia Davis, Transl.). Allen Lane.

Tolkein, J. R. R. (1969). *The Lord of the Rings*. George Allen & Unwin.

WEBSITES

Home page for the urban homestead farm and institute founded by Jules Dervaes Jr.
https://www.urbanhomestead.org/

Website and blog of Peter Adeney, aka Mr. Money Mustache.
https://www.mrmoneymustache.com/

DISCLAIMER

All the events in this book actually happened and all the characters are real. However, the names of people and establishments have been changed for privacy.

Printed in Great Britain
by Amazon